Lonely Planet Kids

create your own

Vacation

GAMES

ACKNOWLEDGEMENTS

Commissioned and project managed by Duck Egg Blue Limited

Author: Laura Baker
Editor: Kait Eaton
Illustrator: Yu Kito Lee
Designers: Duck Egg Blue Limited and Stephen Scanlan
Publisher: Piers Pickard
Editorial Director: Joe Fullman
Commissioning Editor: Kate Baker
Art Director: Andy Mansfield
Print Production: Nigel Longuet

Published in May 2022 by
Lonely Planet Global Limited
CRN: 554153
ISBN: 978 1 83869 515 6
www.lonelyplanet.com/kids
© Lonely Planet 2022

10 9 8 7 6 5 4 3 2 1

Printed in China

STAY IN TOUCH

lonelyplanet.com/contact

Lonely Planet Office:

IRELAND
Digital Depot, Roe Lane (off Thomas St),
Digital Hub, Dublin 8, D08 TCV4, Ireland

MIX
Paper from
responsible sources
FSC™ C021741

Paper in this book is certified against the
Forest Stewardship Council™ standards.
FSC™ promotes environmentally responsible,
socially beneficial and economically viable
management of the world's forests.

lonely planet kids

create your own

Vacation
GAMES

WRITTEN BY LAURA BAKER

ILLUSTRATED BY YU KITO LEE

CONTENTS

DESTINATION: FUN!   6

WHAT YOU'LL NEED   8

ON-THE-GO GAMES   11

FILL THE BUCKET   12
LOTS OF LISTS   14
CAR COUNTING   15
HAND GAMES   16
I SPY   18
TRAIN BINGO   20
ALPHABET GAME   22
RAINBOW GAME   23
GET THE POINT   24
WOULD YOU RATHER?   26
CRAZY QUESTIONS   28
MINI CHALLENGES   30

BRAIN GAMES   33

TRIVIA QUIZ   34
SILLY STORY   36
TEST YOUR MEMORY   38
WORD PLAY   40
I WENT ON VACATION...   42
SECRET SPY   44
20 QUESTIONS   46
TONGUE TWISTERS   48
DON'T SAY THAT!   50
WHICH CUP?   52
CUBE CONUNDRUM   53

PEN-AND-PAPER GAMES   55

CLASSIC PAPER GAMES   56
SPOT THE DIFFERENCE   58
JIGSAW PUZZLES   60
A-MAZE-ING MAZES   62
WORD SEARCH   64
WORD CLUES   65
THE CHALLENGER   66
FILL IN THE GAPS   68
MIX-AND-MATCH MONSTERS   70
PLAY WITH NUMBERS   72
PAPER BOAT RACES   74

OUTDOOR GAMES 99

COURSE OF OBSTACLES 100
STICK GAMES 102
TREASURE QUEST 104
VACATION CHAMPIONSHIPS 106
RELAY RACE 108
TAG TEAM 109
HIDING GAMES 110
HIDE AND FIND 111
BOWLED OVER 112
PAPER AIRPLANES 114
HOPPING HOPSCOTCH 116
MAKE YOUR OWN MINI-GOLF 118

CARD AND BOARD GAMES 77

CLASSIC FUN 78
TRAVEL CARDS 80
SNAKES AND LADDERS 82
ESCAPE ROOM 84
EXPLORER ESCAPADES 86
JUMBO DOMINOES 88
YOUR VACATION GAME 90
WEAVING CHECKERS 92
WHO COULD IT BE? 94
TOP SCORE 96

PARTY GAMES 121

VACATION CHARADES 122
GUESSING GAMES 124
FOREHEAD FUN 126
PICTURE PLAY 128
PAPER CUP GAMES 130
CAPTURE THE FLAG 132
PIN THE PALM 134
DANCING GAMES 136
WHO DID THAT? 138
CLASSICS WITH A TWIST 140

NEVER STOP PLAYING 142

MAKE YOUR OWN DICE 144

DESTINATION: FUN!

The number of players suggested for each game appears in the top corner.

Vacations are full of **excitement and adventure** as you travel somewhere new. Increase the **fun factor** with this book of vacation games. It's bursting with ideas to keep you entertained on the go and at your vacation destination!

Whether you're traveling in a car, train, or plane, or staying at a cabin, campsite, or hotel, we have plenty of ideas for you. You don't need to find any pre-made games stashed in vacation-home closets. Simply grab items from around you, switch on your imagination, and invent your own!

If a game requires any materials to make, you'll find them listed here.

Some games are great for solo entertainment, while others work best with a group. Play alone, or gather family and friends for a challenge. Check the number of players suggested at the top of the page.

Your journey starts here

Journey through the chapters of this book to make and play games on the go, test and train your brain, put pen to paper, try a twist on the classics, get outside, and gather round with party games. At the end of the book, you'll find a dice template and even more ideas and inspiration.

READY, STEADY... MAKE AND PLAY!

PLAYERS 2+

SNAKES LADDER

Start with a grid, then let your imagination **run wild**! Will you try the traditional snakes and ladders or **invent your own**? Prepare to travel up and down in this roller coaster of a game.

You will need
- Letter-sized paper
- Scissors
- Ruler
- Pencil
- Felt-tip pens
- Glue
- Objects to use as tokens, such as different colored buttons, coins, stones, or small toy figures

100	99	98	97	96	95
81	82	83	84	85	86
80	79	78	77	76	
61	62	63	64	66	66
60	59	58	57	56	
41	42	43	44	45	46
40	39	38	37	36	
21	22	23	24	25	26
20	18	18	17	18	
1	2	3	4	5	6

Make your dice

Trace the dice template on page 144. Write the numbers 1 to 6 on the different squares. Cut out, fold, and glue to create a cube.

82

For games that need creating before playing, follow the "How to make" instructions.

Lots of games give extra ideas and tips for ways to invent your own variations.

AND

Learn the rules here!

Invent your own
The key to snakes and ladders is having objects that take you up the board, and others that slide you down. Think about your own version. What could you use instead of ladders and snakes? Slides rather than snakes? Or you could make a space-themed board and have rockets to go up and comets to go down. What can you think up?

100 FINISH	99	98	97	96	95	94			
81	82	83	84	85	86	8			
80	79	78	77	76	75	74			
61	62	63	64	65	66	67	68	69	70
60	59	58	57	56	55	54	53		51
41	42	43	44	45	46	47	48	49	50
40	39	38	37	36	35	34	33	32	31
21	22	23	24	25	26	27	28	29	30
20	19	18	17	16	15	14	13	12	11
1 START	2	3	4	5				9	10

Make sure to put the heads, tails, and ladder tops and bottoms clearly within squares, so you know where they start and end.

How to make

1. Lay the paper flat, short side at the bottom. Fold the top right corner to the left edge.

2. Cut along the bottom line as shown. Open the triangle. You should now have a square.

3. Use your ruler to make marks every 2.1 cm across the page.

4. Draw straight lines down with your ruler and pencil at each of these marks. You should end up with 10 columns.

5. Rotate the paper and repeat steps 3 and 4. You should now have a grid of 100 squares.

6. Write number 1 in the bottom left corner. Then continue numbering each square from 1 to 100, zigzagging up the grid. Square 100 should end up in the top left.

7. Draw snakes and ladders on your board! Place them wherever you like, but space them apart. For snakes, draw a head higher than the tail, so you slide down the snake from head to tail.

How to play

1. Choose a token per player. Place these items on the start square.

2. Roll the dice to decide who goes first. The highest roll starts the game.

3. On a player's turn, they roll the dice, then move their token that many spaces forward.

4. If they land at the bottom of a ladder, they climb to the space at the top. But if they land on a snake's head, they must slide down to its tail!

5. Each player rolls the dice and moves in turn.

6. The first player to reach the finish wins!

83

WHAT YOU'LL NEED

All the games in this book have been carefully chosen and designed to make and play away from home—**on the go or on vacation**. For most of them you don't need much at all. Just bring your **switched-on mind** and a **wild imagination**, and you're ready for action!

Some games make use of simple crafting items you are likely to have around you:

Felt-tip pens or crayons

Scissors

Pencils

Glue stick

Sticky notes

Paint

Ruler

Sticky tape

Timer

Pack prepared
You could plan to pack some paper and pens so you're ready to make at any time!

Cardstock

Paper

Other games use objects that you might find on vacation:

- Plates, bowls, and mugs
- Paper cups
- Empty yogurt containers
- Empty beverage bottles
- Paper towel tubes
- Coins
- Small toys and teddy bears
- Hula hoop
- Jump rope
- Balls
- String
- Blankets
- Buckets
- Sidewalk chalk
- Stones
- Sticks

IT'S YOUR VACATION, AND THESE ARE YOUR VACATION GAMES!

Make it work for you

Check the "You will need" list of each game so you know what materials you should have on hand to make and play.

If you don't have the exact item the instructions call for, improvise with what's around you! Find cardboard from a used or empty box, make playing pieces from stones or spare buttons, a ball from scrunched-up paper, and more.

ON-THE-GO GAMES

The journey has just begun... It's time to start the fun!
Make the time pass along your route with games you
can invent and play in a **car**, or on a **train**, **bus**, or **plane**!
Some of the games in this chapter use a notebook
and pen, while others need only your imagination.
Your vacation-game journey **starts here**.

FILL THE BUCKET

You will need
- Paper
- Felt-tip pens

A bucket list is a list of things that you'd like to do in your life. Start your vacation by making a **vacation bucket list** of things you'd like to do and see on your trip, then **check them off** as you go!

My Vacation Bucket List

How to make and play

1 Draw a large bucket on your piece of paper.

2 On the bucket, write all the things you would like to see and do on your vacation. These could be things that you find on your journey or activities you'll do when you arrive at your destination.

3 Every time that you complete one of the items on your list over the course of your vacation, give it a big checkmark!

How many will you complete?

You do you
The items on your list will depend on where you're going—beach, cabin, city vacation, camping, or wherever! Think carefully about what you might do and see, and what you'd LIKE to do and see. This is your chance to make your own personal wish list. Speak to your family and travel-mates about things they're hoping for on this vacation, too.

**Try these ideas to get started
filling your bucket.**

- [ ] Cross a border
- [ ] Spot a shooting star
- [ ] Skim a stone on the water
- [x] Climb a tree
- [ ] Climb a mountain
- [ ] Play beach volleyball
- [ ] Go for a picnic
- [ ] Surf a wave
- [ ] Eat something new
- [x] Write in a journal
- [x] Find a four-leaf clover
- [ ] Ride a roller coaster
- [x] Catch (and release) a crab
- [x] Find a fossil
- [ ] Build an outdoor shelter
- [ ] Watch the sunrise
- [x] Build a sandcastle
- [x] Travel in a canoe
- [ ] Speak to someone from somewhere different

LOTS OF LISTS

Keep your **eyes peeled** on your travels! Create some lists, then see
how many items you can **add to them** before the journey ends.

You will need
- Paper
- Felt-tip pens

Things that are green	Things with legs	Things that make a noise	Things with wheels
grass	cat	police car	car
tree	dog	bird	bus
bush	pedestrian	car horn	horse trailer
green car	spider		camper van
green traffic light	cow		bicycle

How to make and play

1 At the beginning of your journey, draw vertical lines to divide your paper into four columns.

2 Write a category at the top of each column, such as "things that are green," "things with legs," "things that make a noise," and "things with wheels."

3 Then start searching! Look out the window and write down anything you see that fits into one of the columns.

4 Can you complete the sheet before you arrive at your destination?

Healthy competition
If you are playing with other people, have each person write up a list. See who can spot the most items in each category before the end of the journey!

CAR COUNTING

Race to **count cars** before you reach your destination. This game is best played on **road trips**, but you could adapt it to suit your mode of transportation.

You will need
- Paper
- Felt-tip pens

How to play

1 Each person chooses a different color of car.

2 Throughout the journey, players count each car of their chosen color that they see. Create a tally chart to help keep track if you like.

3 Who has spotted the most cars by the journey's end?

Wacky wild car

To bump up the difficulty, you could add a "wild car," such as a white car. Count as many cars in your chosen color as you can—but when you pass a white car on your side of the vehicle, your count must reset to zero. Then start counting from one again!

Player	Color	Cars spotted
Mom		~~HHT~~ ~~HHT~~ II
Nan		~~HHT~~ III
Hugo		~~HHT~~ ~~HHT~~ ~~HHT~~ ~~HHT~~ I Winner!
Emilia		IIII

HAND GAMES

These are great games to have **on hand** when you want to pass some time on a journey. No equipment needed! Simply **challenge a friend** and use your hands to play.

ROCK, PAPER, SCISSORS

In this game, there are three hand signals to choose from:

Rock – dulls scissors
Scissors – cut paper
Paper – covers rock

Each player makes a fist with their right hand. Count to three. On each count, tap your fist against your left palm. After three, make any of the three hand shapes with your right hand at the same time as the other player. Determine who wins! If you both make the same shape, it's a tie, so try again.

You could play this as the best out of three or keep going until you get bored!

Paper covers rock

Rock

Rock dulls scissors

Paper

Scissors

Scissors cut paper

Invent your own

What other versions of this game can you think up? You'll need three objects that you can form with your hand, and each one should have a way to beat one of the others.

For example:

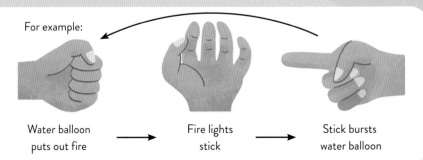

Water balloon puts out fire → Fire lights stick → Stick bursts water balloon

THUMB WAR

Clasp your fingers with the other player, thumbs up. Then recite the traditional opening:

> **ONE, TWO, THREE, FOUR,
> I DECLARE A THUMB WAR.
> BOW, KISS, HUG, BEGIN!**

Bow (bend your thumb to bow to the other person)

Kiss (touch thumb pads)

Hug (cross thumbs)

Keeping your hands as still as possible, use only your thumb to try to pin down the other player's thumb. The first person to hold down the other player's thumb for five seconds wins.

Winner!

Invent your own

There are lots of variations on the rhyme that starts a thumb war.

"One, two, three, four,
I declare a thumb war.
Five, six, seven, eight,
try to keep your thumb straight!"

Can you make up your own rhyme?

BACK PICTURES

A CUP?

Player 1 turns away from player 2, with their back facing player 2. Player 2 uses their finger to draw a picture on player 1's back. Player 1 must guess what it is! You could give clues or categories, such as food, animals, or vacation items, to help. You could also play this game drawing letters to write secret messages to the other person.

I SPY

What can you spy as the scenery rushes by? Play this **classic travel game**, then make up your own versions. Keep an **eye out!**

You will need
- Paper
- Felt-tip pens

How to play

1 One player is the spotter. They choose something that everyone else can see (and that won't disappear too quickly if you travel past it).

2 The spotter says, "I spy with my little eye something that is..." and fills in the sentence with a description of their mystery item. For example, if the spotter chooses the clouds, they could say, "I spy with my little eye something that is white and fluffy."

3 All the other players shout out guesses.

4 When one person guesses correctly, they become the spotter, and the game starts again.

Add rules

Think about ways to make the game more challenging. For example:

- Limit the mystery objects to things that are inside or outside of your vehicle.
- Allow each player only three guesses. They need to think carefully before they shout them out!
- Let each player ask three yes or no questions before they guess.

THAT CLOUD SHAPED LIKE A SNAKE?

A STREAM?

THE ROAD?

Invent your own

What other descriptions could you use for your game? Try using the first letter of your mystery object and say for example, "I spy with my little eye something beginning with L" (answer: lake). You could decide that everyone must use colors only, or shapes to describe their mystery object. Or you could say that they CAN'T use colors and must describe their object another way—the sillier the better!

TRAIN BINGO

You will need
- Paper
- Ruler
- Pencil
- Felt-tip pens

This game combines things that **might happen**, items you **could spot**, and **playful challenges** in a fun, competitive way. Make your own boards, then see who can yell **"Bingo!"** first.

How to make

1 Use your ruler and pencil to draw six vertical lines on a sheet of paper. This should divide it into five columns.

2 Now draw six horizontal lines on your paper. This should give you five rows and a grid of 25 squares.

3 In the center square, draw a star. This is a free space. This space counts as one of your completed squares.

4 In the other 24 squares, write something that could happen on your trip. If you're in an airplane, it could be "the seatbelt sign goes on." If you're on a train, you could write "hear the train horn."

5 Repeat steps 1 to 4 to make a bingo sheet for each of the people playing. Write the items on the board in different spaces, so no two boards are identical. You could write different items on each board, too.

How to play

As you travel along, try to complete or spot the items on your board. Check each one with your felt-tip pens as you do. Once you complete a line of five (across, down, or diagonally), shout out "Bingo!" The first person to call out bingo is the winner.

Give yourself challenges to complete on your journey.

Hear the train horn	Stop at a signal	Laugh at a joke the driver makes over the loudspeaker	Read a book on the train	Sing a song about trains
Show your ticket to the conductor	See a dog on the train	Sit facing backward	Smile at a stranger	Eat a snack while the train is moving
Go through a tunnel	Go through a station with a name starting with M	FREE SPACE	Have a nap	See someone board with a bicycle
Draw a train picture	Play I Spy	Walk up and down the aisle	Spot something orange	Ask the conductor a question about their job
Say thank you to someone deserving	Write a poem about your vacation	Spot a wild animal out the window	Shout "choo-choo!"	Wave to someone watching the train from outside

Catchphrase catch-out

Write travel catchphrases in the squares instead of actions. These are things you might hear people say on your journey, such as "Are we nearly there yet?", "I'm hungry", and "Does anyone need the bathroom?". Each time you hear someone say one of these phrases, check it off your bingo board.

ARE WE NEARLY THERE YET?

ALPHABET GAME

Follow a specific order to **step up the difficulty of** your spotting games. Use the **alphabet or colors of the rainbow** and see who you can stump!

How to play

1 The youngest player goes first. They spot something around them beginning with the letter A, such as an airplane. They must point to it and say its name.

2 The next youngest player spots and names an object beginning with B.

3 The next player spots and names an object beginning with C, and so on, with players taking turns to spot an object in the order of each letter of the alphabet.

4 If a player can't find anything for their letter, they're out of the game. Who can make it to the end?

Note: For a friendlier version, you could allow a player to pass if they can't think of an object. They skip their turn, and the next person takes their letter. Then the game continues.

You might need to get creative if you're having trouble spotting things for certain letters. Try using adjectives, or describing words, to help.

A VERY NICE HAT

Can you find something for every letter of the alphabet?

V

X

X-TRAORDINARY STATUES

AN UNUSUAL TREE

U

You could also spot the letters themselves on car license plates or signs.

SKY

TREE

GET THE POINT!

You will need
- Notebook or a piece of paper
- Pen or pencil

Take **spotting games** to the next level by **adding points**. Who can rack up the **highest score** before the journey ends?

How to play

1 On the paper, write a list of fun things you might spot on your journey. Think of simple things that you see all the time and other things that are very rare to spot.

2 For each item, assign a points value from 1 to 5. Give fewer points, such as 1 or 2, to things that are easy to spot. Items that are hard to spot should get the full 5 points.

3 On your journey, look for the items on your list. Make a chart to keep track of each person's spots. Whenever someone sees something, write down the number of points of that item in their column. When you reach your destination, add up each player's points. Whoever has the highest score wins!

green moped

Add specific descriptions to make spotting things trickier!

Here are some ideas to start you off...

telephone pole — **1**

yellow car — **4**

town beginning with B — **B.....** **2**

wind turbine — **2**

ginger cat — **2**

helicopter — **3**

airplane — **2**

green moped — **4**

man with a hat — **2**

dog wearing a sweater — **5**

flashing light — **3**

bird in a tree — **3**

tow truck — **3**

gas station — **1**

donut shop — DONUTS **4**

coach — **2**

red tractor — **2**

power station — **5**

train — **3**

cement mixer — **4**

	Mom	Mya	Dylan
	2	3	2
	2	2	2
	2	1	1
	3	2	3
	4		5
			3
Total	13	8	16

If you are playing by yourself, see if you can get more than 20 points before the journey ends.

TOP SPOTTER!

WOULD YOU RATHER?

Make some **tough choices** with these **this-or-that** questions. Would you rather fly or sail? Would you rather go on a tropical vacation or a city vacation? **You decide!**

WOULD YOU RATHER VISIT YOUR FAVORITE PLACE OR TRAVEL SOMEWHERE NEW?

How to play

1 The oldest player goes first. They ask any other player a "would you rather" question, such as "Would you rather blast into space or dive to the deepest part of the ocean?"

2 The player who has been asked answers the question. There is no wrong answer, but they must choose one of the options. No ties or passes allowed! They can explain their answer if they want to.

3 Once they've answered the question, they ask a new question to someone else.

4 Continue for as long as you like! Make the questions sillier or trickier as you go.

Question quest

To make up a question, put two similar but different things together. Think about your vacation, too.

For example:
Would you rather sleep under the stars or underground?

Would you rather be barefoot in Antarctica or wearing a parka in the Amazon?

The questions could include two things that would both be fun to do, or two things that would both be very awkward! This could make it a tough choice.

WOULD YOU RATHER...

Try these questions to get you started. What others can you add to the list? Let your imagination run wild!

TRAVEL TO THE PAST OR TO THE FUTURE?

FUTURE!

CLIMB A MOUNTAIN OR KAYAK ON A RIVER?

CLIMB A MOUNTAIN.

SLEEP ON THE GROUND OR SLEEP IN A TREE?

SLEEP IN A TREE.

EAT PIZZA ALL DAY OR EAT ICE CREAM ALL NIGHT?

PIZZA ALL DAY!

HAVE NO BOOKS OR NO TV?

NO TV.

A DRAGON!

BY THE SEA.

FLY ON A MAGIC CARPET OR ON A DRAGON?

STAY IN THE WOODS OR STAY BY THE SEA?

Now add your own!

WOULD YOU RATHER EAT A BUG SANDWICH OR TOUCH A SLIPPERY SNAKE?

TOUCH A SNAKE!

Chitchat
Instead of just one person answering a question, have all the players say what they'd rather do. This could get a good debate going, too.

27

CRAZY QUESTIONS

It's time to **get to know each other** better! Find out more about your friends and family using open-ended questions. Will you be **surprised** at their answers?

How to play

1 The oldest player goes first. They ask a question to the group, such as "Where would you most like to go on vacation?"

2 All the other players take turns to answer the question honestly.

3 Take turns to ask more questions. Keep going for as long as you like!

WHAT IS THE BRAVEST THING YOU'VE EVER DONE?

RIDING A HUGE ROLLER COASTER!

Step it up

At the end of the game, you could add the challenge of remembering what other people have said. The first player describes the player to their left, using as many answers as they can remember. For example, player 1 could say, "This is Theo. He would most like to go on vacation to Mount Everest, he has been as far as Paris...," and so on. Theo then describes the person to his left. Continue until each player has described one other person. Who can remember the most facts about the other players?

MINI CHALLENGES

Every time there's a pause in your journey, try a **mini challenge!** Dare family members to join in, too, and see who can come out **on top** in these **quick contests.**

Star jumps
Best played at: a highway rest area, bus station, or train station.
How many star jumps can you do in one minute? Challenge your family! Who can complete the most?

Name game
Best played at: a red light or while a train is stopped at a station.
Ask someone else to count how many times you can say your name over and over before the break ends (e.g. before the light turns green or the train starts moving again).

Follow the leader
Best played at: a highway rest area (on the grass) or a scenic viewpoint.
Appoint one person as the leader. Follow the leader, marching, skipping, crawling, and more around the grass. At the next rest area, choose a different leader!

Color competition

Best played: anywhere!

Ask one person to choose a color. The race is on... who can spot something in that color first? The first person to shout out an object of that color picks the next color. Continue with the game until your break is over.

ORANGE

TRAFFIC CONES!

Quick call

Best played at: a red light, while the train is stopped at a station, or while the airplane seatbelt sign is on.

Ask an adult to call out instructions, one after the other quite quickly. For example, they could say, "Touch your nose! Wiggle your ears! Pat your head!" and so on. Can you keep up?

Invent your own

What other challenges can you invent? When you're stuck in traffic or at a break in your travel, think up things to do to get everyone moving and laughing. Take turns making up challenges and calling out super-quick mini-games.

Dance party

This last one is just for fun! Blast the tunes while you're stuck in traffic, and get everyone boogying in their seats. What crazy on-the-go moves can you make up?

BRAIN GAMES

Just because you're on vacation doesn't mean that your brain has to be! Keep your mind in gear with **baffling brain-benders** and **tricky teasers**. Play these games on your journey or at your destination if you've got some downtime. Who is feeling super-sharp, and who is stuck in vacation mode? It's time for the **battle of the brains**!

TRIVIA QUIZ

Test your knowledge and **learn something new** with a fun quiz for all the family. Stick to the vacation theme with an **around-the-world** game. Then make up questions in other favorite categories!

You will need (optional)
- Paper
- Pens

How to play

Take turns asking each other a trivia question about the world. Go with info that you know, or look in books and online to find fun facts. Who can shout out the correct answer first?

Try these fun-fact questions to get you started...

What is the capital of England? **London.**

Where is the highest point on Earth? **Mount Everest.**

What is the largest ocean? **The Pacific Ocean.**

How many continents are there? **Seven.**

What is the biggest mammal on the planet? **The blue whale.**

How many people live on planet Earth? **Over 7 billion!**

How many people live on Antarctica permanently? **Zero.**

How many states are in the United States of America? **Fifty.**

COUNTLESS CATEGORIES

Think of other categories for your questions. Choose something that you all know about, such as:

Movie mania
Pick a favorite film and ask each other questions about the characters, the story, the setting, and more.

Family fun
Make up questions about your own family! What color are your grandma's eyes? What is Dad's favorite food? Who has visited Mexico? See if you can stump each other!

Sports superstars
Do you all follow a favorite sport? Ask each other questions about the players, recent games, and the sport's history.

TEAM COMPETITION

For a more formal trivia game, split into two teams. Each team writes down 10 trivia questions, with their answers. Start the timer for two minutes.

One team asks the other team the first question from their paper. The other team answers as quickly as they can. If they get the answer correct, mark 1 point on your paper and move on to the next question. If they get it wrong, move on to the next question. The team can also say "pass" to skip a question if they don't know the answer.

Stop when the timer is up. Then swap! The other team asks the first team their questions in the same way. After both rounds, the team with the most points wins!

SILLY STORY

Switch on your imagination and **get creative!**
Work together to make up a really silly story.
What **wild adventure** will you create?

You will need (optional)
- Paper
- Pens

> ONCE UPON A TIME THERE WAS A DRAGON CALLED FLUFF.

How to play

1 Player 1 makes up one sentence of a story. They say it out loud to the rest of the group.

2 Player 2 adds the next sentence.

3 Player 3 (or back to Player 1 if you have only two players) adds the next sentence.

4 Continue taking turns to add a sentence to the story until you reach its end.

> FLUFF RAN AWAY TO TRY TO ESCAPE THE FIRE.

> SHE FLEW SO FAR THAT SHE GOT TO ICY ANTARCTICA.

> SHE MET SOME GIRAFFES WHO LOOKED VERY COLD.

SECRET STORY

To make things even sillier, try this variation. Keep your story hidden until the grand reveal at the end.

1. The first person writes their line at the top of a piece of paper.

2. The next player writes a line below the first. They then fold the paper over backward to hide the first line.

3. The next player reads the one line they can see. They add a line below, then fold the top line back so it's hidden.

4. Continue in this way, reading just the one line visible, adding another, and folding back the top line.

5. When the paper is full, unfold it. Read out the story from the beginning!

FLUFF WAS NOT A VERY SCARY DRAGON.

FLUFF WAS SCARED OF LOTS OF THINGS—EVEN HER OWN FIRE.

ONE DAY, SHE SNEEZED AND SOME FIRE BLASTED OUT.

SHE WAS BRAVE AND KIND AND BREATHED FIRE TO WARM THEM UP.

FLUFF REALIZED FIRE WASN'T SO SCARY AFTER ALL!

AFTER HER ADVENTURE, FLUFF WASN'T SCARED OF ANYTHING ANY MORE—EXCEPT MAYBE KNIGHTS.

THEY HAD RUN AWAY, TOO!

TEST YOUR MEMORY

Train your brain with a memory game! Look closely at some objects, then try to remember them when they're gone. Will any **slip your mind?**

You will need
- Tray or plate
- 10 objects from around you, such as a small toy, a button, a leaf, a colored pencil, a key, and a sock
- A timer
- A napkin or cloth
- Paper
- Pencils

How to play

1 Lay out the 10 objects on the tray. Place the tray on a table.

2 Study the tray for 30 seconds.

3 After the 30 seconds are up, cover the tray with the napkin or cloth.

4 Each player writes on their piece of paper every object they can remember.

5 Who can remember the most? Use more objects to make the game even harder!

What's missing?

For a sneaky variation of this game, close your eyes and have an adult take away one object from the tray after you've all studied it for 30 seconds. Open your eyes. Who can figure out which item is missing?

Super simple

If you're playing this game on the road or while you're out exploring, you could simply use a notebook and pencil rather than actual things. Draw 10 or more random objects on a piece of paper. Study it for 30 seconds, then close your notebook. Work together as a team to try to name all 10 things!

WORD PLAY

Think fast as you play with words and letters. Try these games in a vacation home or on the road. All you need is more than one player and some **switched-on brains!**

WORD TO WORD

Sit in a circle and choose a player to go first. The first player says a random word. The person to their left shouts out the first word that comes to mind connected to this word. The next player in the circle shouts out a word connected to the previous one, and so on. Continue around the circle, creating a chain of words. If a player can't think of a word or repeats a word already used, the game ends. Try again with a new starting word, and see if you can create an even longer chain!

START

DOG

CAT

BONE

ISLAND

DIG

TREASURE

WOOF!
WOOF!

PLACE CHASE

Choose a player to go first. They name a place—a city, town, or country anywhere in the world. The next player must then name a place that starts with the last letter of the first place named. For example, if the first player says "Paris," the next player must choose a place starting with S, such as San Francisco. The player after that must think of a place starting with O, such as Oman. The game continues until a player is stuck or repeats a place name already used. Then the game can start again with a new word!

Can you invent other categories for this game? You could try making a chain of animal names, food items, or even family names!

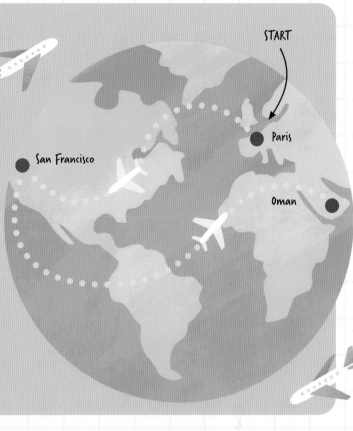

START

Paris

San Francisco

Oman

ONE, TWO, THREE, FOUR, FIVE...

...FIVE LITTLE MONKEYS JUMPING ON THE...

SING IT!

Add some melody to your games! For this word game, brush up on your song lyrics. The first player must sing a line of a song, such as:

"One, two, three, four, five..."

Any player can then jump in and start a new lyric using the word at the end of the first player's line as the first word of their line, such as:

"Five little monkeys jumping on the..."

Another player jumps in and picks up on a word to start their line, such as:

"The wheels on the bus go round and round..."

Lines can be from any song you like—nursery rhymes, pop songs, songs from films, or whatever you can think of! Continue until you run out of matches. Then play again!

I WENT ON VACATION...

Not only is this game great fun for vacation giggles, but it's also perfect for **training your brain**. How far can you get in the list?

How to play

1 Sit in a circle, or choose an order of players if you're on the road.

2 The first player says, "I went on vacation, and I packed...," then adds one item that they packed, such as a toothbrush.

3 The next player or the player to their left must repeat the first player's line as they said it and then add one more item. For example, they could say, "I went on vacation, and I packed a toothbrush and toothpaste."

4 The next player repeats the line with all the items and adds one more of their own, such as "I went on vacation, and I packed a toothbrush, toothpaste, and a swimsuit."

5 Continue taking turns repeating the sentence with all previous items, plus adding a new one.

6 If a player can't remember all the items or misses one from the list, they're out of the game.

7 See how far can you get!

I WENT ON VACATION, AND I PACKED A TOOTHBRUSH, TOOTHPASTE, A HAT, A CAMERA, SUNGLASSES...

Tip: Add items in alphabetical order so they're easier to remember!

DANCE IT!

1 Try the list game with a series of dance moves to perform instead of items to recite. This one is best done standing up!

2 Stand in a circle. Player 1 makes up a short dance move, such as waving their arms.

3 The person to the left copies this dance move, then adds their own. For example, they wave their arms and then could add a slide.

4 The next person copies the previous moves and adds their own. For example, they would do an arm wave, a slide, and then could add a knee bend.

5 Continue taking turns repeating all the previous moves and adding your own.

6 If someone forgets a move, they're out. Who is the last dancer standing?

Move to the beat
Find some fun tunes and match your moves to the music!

SECRET SPY

Become **secret spies** for the day and communicate cryptically. Make up codes, then pass them to your partner agent to decode. **Your mission** is to keep them secret from everyone else!

SECRET CODE

How to play

1 Write the alphabet across your page. If you go over to the next line, be sure to leave an empty line in between.

2 Under each letter, draw a different symbol, such as a star, swirl, or dot. To keep it simpler, you could also just write the alphabet again backward or use numbers.

3 Now write your secret message! For every letter that you need to write, refer to your code and write the letter, number, or symbol beneath.

4 Secretly slip your secret message and the code to your partner. They will have to check what each symbol means on your chart to decode the message.

A	B	C	D	E	F	G
✱	✱✱	+	○	†	✕	●

H	I	J	K	L	M	N
◆	△	✳	❋	◈	⊠	✂

O	P	Q	R	S	T	U
◖	■	▣	◖	≈	⏶	◡

V	W	X	Y	Z
⊙	⊗	☑	✓	🏷

Solve this message:

☑ † † ⏶   ☑ †   ✱ ⏶   ⏶ ◆ †   ● ✱ ⏶ †

SPIRAL CIPHER

You will need

- Paper
- Scissors
- Sticky tape or adhesive putty
- Pen
- Paper towel tube, rolling pin, pencil, or another long cylinder

How to play

THE JEWEL
IS IN THE
PIANO

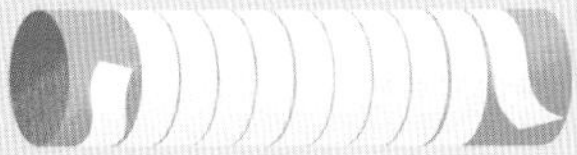

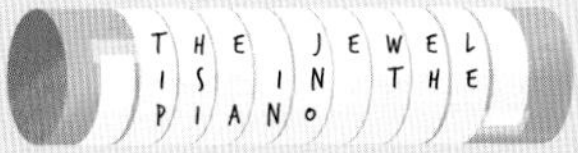

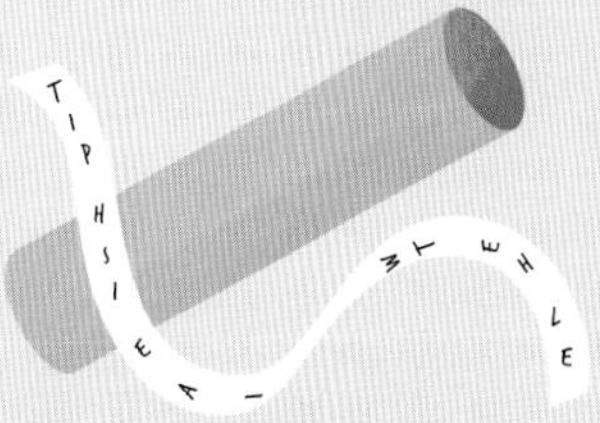

1 Cut a thin strip off the long edge of your paper. Wrap the paper around your cylinder, starting at the left end.

2 Lightly stick each end in place, using sticky tape or adhesive putty. Write your message straight across the piece of paper, placing one letter in each section of the strip, as shown above.

3 Carefully unstick the ends of the paper. Unroll the strip. Secretly pass the strip of paper and the cylinder to your partner. They must wrap the paper around the tube to decode the message!

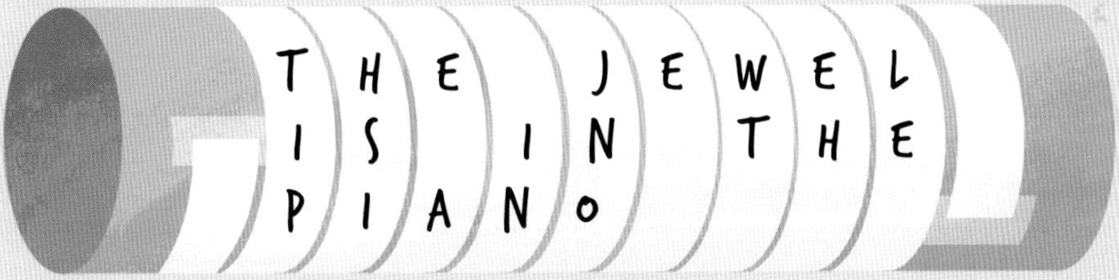

THE JEWEL
IS IN THE
PIANO

Only a spy with the exact same tube as you will be able to read your message. To anyone else it will look like random letters!

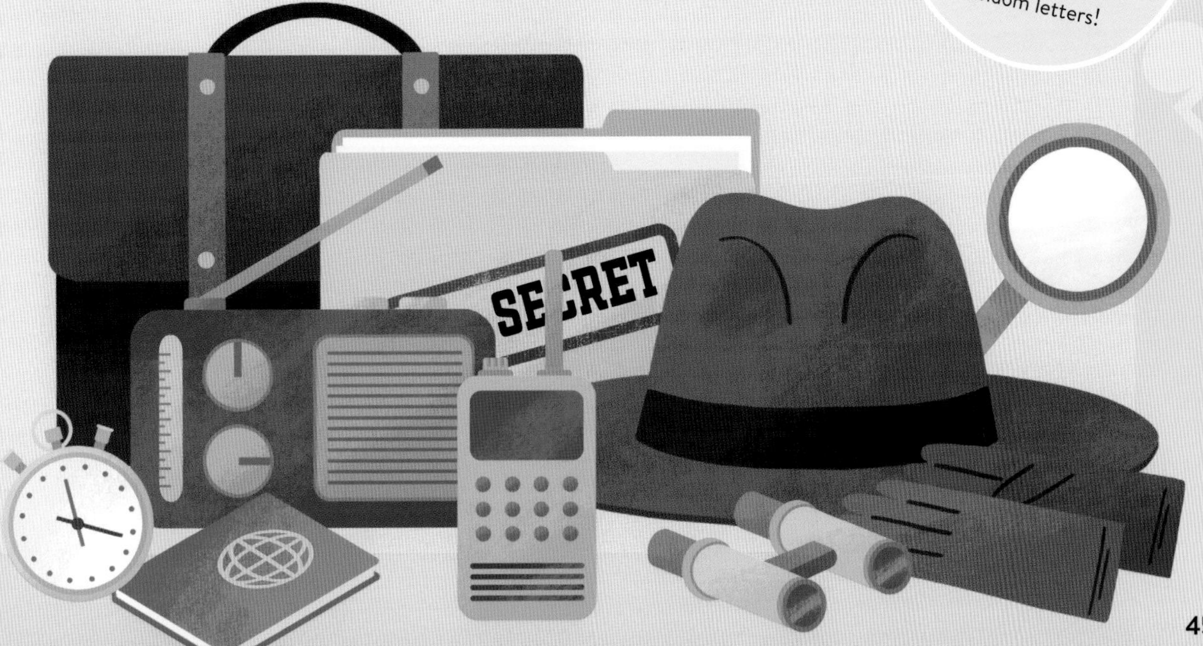

SECRET

20 QUESTIONS

Using only **yes or no** questions, can you figure out what someone is thinking? You have 20 questions to **read their mind!**

How to play

1 One player thinks of a place. They keep it to themselves.

2 The other players take turns asking questions about the place. You must be able to answer these questions with a simple "yes" or "no" (or "I don't know"). For example, you could ask, "Is the place a city?" but not "Where is the place?"

3 Keep count of the questions you ask. If you think you know the answer, take a guess! This will count as one of your questions if you get it wrong.

4 Once you've asked 20 questions, you must stop asking and make your final guess. If you're playing with more than one player, each person takes one guess. Did anyone figure it out? If so, that player chooses a new secret word for the next round. If no one guesses correctly, the player can reveal the answer, and they choose a new word.

5 Play again!

1
IS THE PLACE A COUNTRY?
NO.

8
IS IT THE COLOSSEUM?
NO.

9
IS IT IN THE UK?
NO.

Category game

You could choose any category for this game, as long as everyone is familiar with it. Instead of a place, you could choose an animal, food, vacation item, famous person, or even a member of your family. Just make sure everyone knows what the category is before you start!

TONGUE TWISTERS

A **tongue twister** is a group of words with similar sounds that are very hard to say out loud quickly and accurately. Try these tricky twisters, then make up your own. Will you get your **tongue in a tangle**?

FAMOUS PHRASES

Try these tricky twisters to warm up. Read them out loud slowly, and then try saying them as quickly as you can. Can you say each one three times in a row without getting in a muddle? For an extra challenge, try speeding up as you go!

SHE SELLS SEASHELLS BY THE SEASHORE.

SHE SEES CHEESY STRINGS.

PETER PIPER PICKED A PECK OF PICKLED PEPPERS.

RED TRUCK, YELLOW TRUCK.

Similar sounds

To make up your own tongue twisters, think of words that have similar sounds. Then mix these up so your mouth has to keep changing shape—this is what makes it hilariously hard!

For example:

SHE   SURELY   SHALL

SEE   SUN

SOON

Put them together into a sentence:

SHE SURELY SHALL SEE THE SUN SOON.

Take turns and see who can say their tongue twisters the fastest!

Does your mouth try to say "she surely shall shee the sun shoon"?

Your turn

Try these similar-sounding words to get you started, then brainstorm your own. Put them together into tongue-twisting sentences. Challenge a friend or family member to repeat them three times!

big	pip	witch
black	pick	which
bear	purple	watch
blueberries	plum	watched
blended	please	watching
bush	pluck	was

DON'T SAY THAT!

Think before you speak in these quick-witted word swap games. Just remember, **don't say the forbidden words!**

OINK

5

65

SIXTY-OINK

COUNTING CHALLENGE

How to play

1 Choose three silly words to replace three digits. You could use animal sounds, such as "moo" for the number 3, "oink" for the number 5, and "baa" for the number 7.

2 Every time your count comes to 3, 5, or 7, you must say these sounds instead!

3 Decide on an order of players. Player 1 starts counting and says "one." Player 2 continues and says "two." Player 3 counts next, but instead of number three, they say "moo."

4 Continue taking turns to count up, one number at a time. Every time you reach the numbers that have been given silly word substitutes, say these instead. For example, you would say "twenty-two," "twenty-moo," "twenty-four," "twenty-oink," "twenty-six," "twenty-baa," and so on.

5 If someone makes a mistake, they're out! Or, start the game over to try again as a team.

How far can you get?

FORTY-BAA

47

TWENTY-MOO

17

BAA-TEEN

23

FORBIDDEN WORDS

How to play

1 Choose two words or phrases and make them off limits. For example, you could choose the words "fun" and "family."

2 Tell a story about your favorite vacation ever. The only catch is, you can't say the off-limits words as you speak!

3 The other players must listen closely. Can they catch you using the forbidden words?

4 When your story is over, choose two new off-limits words or phrases, and another player can tell their story.

Trio trick

For another version, gather three players, including you. The first person sets the rules. They decide on an item that the second player must describe, such as a television, and three words that are off limits, such as "screen," "watch," and "program." The second player must describe the item without using the off-limits words, and the third player must guess the mystery item!

DID YOU TAKE LOTS OF PHOTOS?

DID YOU HAVE A GOOD TIME?

TOO MANY!

DID YOU GO SURFING?

I SURE DID!

IT WAS TOO COLD.

Step it up
Turn this into a question game, and make your off-limits words "yes" and "no." The other players now ask you questions about your favorite vacation, and you must answer without saying these two words!

DID YOU GO WITH YOUR FAMILY?

DID YOU SLEEP IN A TENT?

I LOVED SLEEPING IN A TENT!

I WENT WITH MOM, NANA, AND MY SISTER.

WOULD YOU GO AGAIN?

OF COURSE!

51

PLAYERS
2+

WHICH CUP?

Test your **concentration and focus** in this cup-moving game. Watch closely and don't take your eyes off the cups for a **single second**!

> Move the cups faster or slower to make the game more or less challenging.

You will need
- Ping-pong ball or scrunched-up piece of paper
- 3 opaque paper cups (not see-through)

How to play

1 Set yourself up at a table in front of the other players. Place the three cups upside down in a row.

2 Tell your audience to watch as you place the ball under one of the cups.

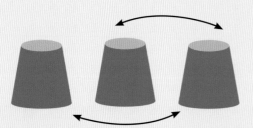

3 Carefully shuffle the cups around, sliding them along the table to switch their positions, keeping the ball securely hidden underneath. The audience must keep their eye closely on the cup that has the ball inside.

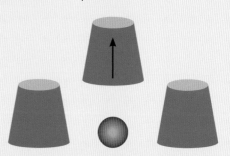

4 When you stop moving the cups, have the other players point out as a group where they think the ball is. Lift up that cup. Were they right?

CUBE CONUNDRUM

This 3D challenge is sure to **stretch your mind** and keep you busy on a rainy day. Can you **work together** to solve the puzzle?

You will need
- 4 pieces of paper, any color
- Pen
- Scissors
- Glue

How to play

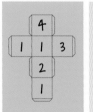

1 Trace the dice template on page 144 on to four separate pieces of paper. Write the numbers 1 to 4 on the faces exactly as shown above.

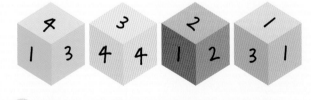

2 Cut out, fold, and glue each paper into a cube shape.

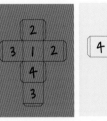

If you're getting stuck, reduce the game to figuring out only two sides of the tower. Take your time!

3 Work together to stack the cubes on top of each other so that each side of the tower shows the numbers 1, 2, 3, and 4. They can be in any order, but each number must appear only once. You'll need to turn the cubes to figure this out. It's harder than it looks!

Solution (numbers top to bottom): **Side one:** 3, 4, 2, 1, **Side two:** 2, 4, 1, 3, **Side three:** 1, 2, 3, 4, **Side four:** 4, 1, 3, 2

PEN-AND-PAPER GAMES

Put **pen to paper** for some serious fun. These games are great for downtime, early mornings, and rainy days indoors during your vacation. Just find some spare paper or cardstock, then spot, puzzle, and work your way through. Make your own games, and challenge your friends and family. Who dares take on your **tricky tasks**?

CLASSIC PAPER GAMES

Let's start with the classics. Find a worthy opponent, a piece of paper, and two pens. Then **let the games begin**!

SNOWMAN

You will need
- Paper
- Pens (one for each of you)

How to play

1 Choose one player to be the chooser and the other to be the guesser. The chooser thinks of a word or phrase. It could be any word at all, or a word related to your vacation.

2 The chooser draws short dashes across the bottom of the page, using one dash for each letter in their word. For example, if they are thinking of the phrase "beach ball," they draw five dashes, followed by a space, followed by four more dashes.

3 The guesser guesses any letter of the alphabet. If the letter is in the word, the chooser writes it in position on the dashes. If there are more than one of the letter guessed, write the letter in each space where it should appear.

B? B _ _ _ _   B _ _ _ _

4 If the letter is not in the word, the chooser draws one part of a snowman on the paper. Continue guessing one letter at a time and adding the letter to the dashes or a part to the snowman.

5 The aim of the game is to guess the word before drawing a complete snowman.

Note: A traditional snowman with three body parts, two eyes, one nose, two arms, and a hat gives you nine guesses. If you want the game to last longer, just add more to your snowperson! Draw a scarf, buttons, fingers... anything you like to keep the game going!

TIC-TAC-TOE

How to play

1 Draw a grid on your paper, using two vertical lines and two horizontal lines. This will give you nine squares.

2 Decide on one person to be O and the other to be X.

3 The youngest player goes first. They draw their symbol (O or X) in one box on the grid.

4 The next player takes a turn and draws their symbol in another box on the grid. Continue taking turns to draw your O or X in a space on the grid.

5 The first person to create a line of three Os or Xs wins! The line can go across, down, or diagonally.

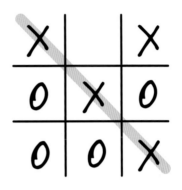

Invent your own
Instead of Os and Xs, you could each choose your own symbol to draw. Stars and hearts? Cats and dogs? You decide!

DOTS AND BOXES

How to play

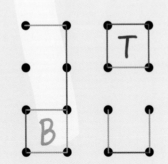

1 Draw a grid of 4x4 dots. The oldest player goes first. They draw one straight line horizontally or vertically (but not diagonally) to connect two dots.

2 The next player draws a line to connect two dots. Continue taking turns to draw a line. Each time you complete a square, write your initial inside the box, then take another turn.

3 Once all the dots are connected, count the initials for each person. Whoever has the higher number of initials on the board (closed the most boxes) wins!

Giant grid
To make the game more challenging (and to make it last longer), draw a bigger grid. How large are you willing to go?

SPOT THE DIFFERENCE

Take your time creating a spot the difference challenge for a friend or family member. Sneak in **10 tricky differences** in one of the images, and see if your opponent can **spot them all**!

You will need
- A sheet of letter-sized paper
- Colored pencils
- Scissors
- Sticky tape
- Eraser

How to make

1 Lay your paper on the table, short side down. Fold it in half from top to bottom, and crease.

2 Open the paper. It should now be divided in two by the crease. Draw a vacation image in the bottom half. Put in lots of details!

How to play

Challenge a friend to
find all 10 differences.

For an extra
challenge, give your
friend a time limit!

Removing an object entirely
from the right-hand image is
sure to stump spotters!

When you color the image, you could
make some things different colors
than they are on the left.

Change details
for a sneaky
variation.

3 Fold the paper in half again.
Trace over the image you drew so that
you make an exact copy.

4 Unfold the paper, then cut
along the crease. Place the images
side by side and tape them together.

5 Use your pencils and eraser
to make 10 differences to your new
picture, then color both images.

JIGSAW PUZZLES

A puzzle is the perfect pastime for **quiet vacation moments**. Make your own, then see if you or a friend can **piece it back together**!

How to make and play

1 Use the glue stick to completely cover one side of the cardstock. Glue the paper to the card, lining up the edges and pressing down securely.

2 Draw a picture on the sheet of paper. Color it in.

Instead of using your ruler, you could draw wobbly lines.

3 Use your ruler and pencil to draw three vertical lines and two horizontal lines evenly spaced out on the cardstock.

4 Carefully cut along the lines. You should end up with 12 puzzle pieces. Now put the puzzle back together! Or give it to someone else to try.

Store your puzzle pieces in a bag, envelope, or box. You could decorate the box and label it with your puzzle's name, too!

Scuba Puzzle

A-MAZE-ING MAZES

You will need
- Paper
- Felt-tip pens

Create a **winding pathway** for a friend or family member to navigate. Can they make it through? Design maze after maze for **a-maze-ing fun**!

Think of a theme

Think of a theme for your maze, and a backstory, too. Who needs to get where? You could have an explorer creeping through the trees to his tent, a bus trying to get to its destination along busy city streets, or a lion cub needing to find its way across the savannah to its mom.

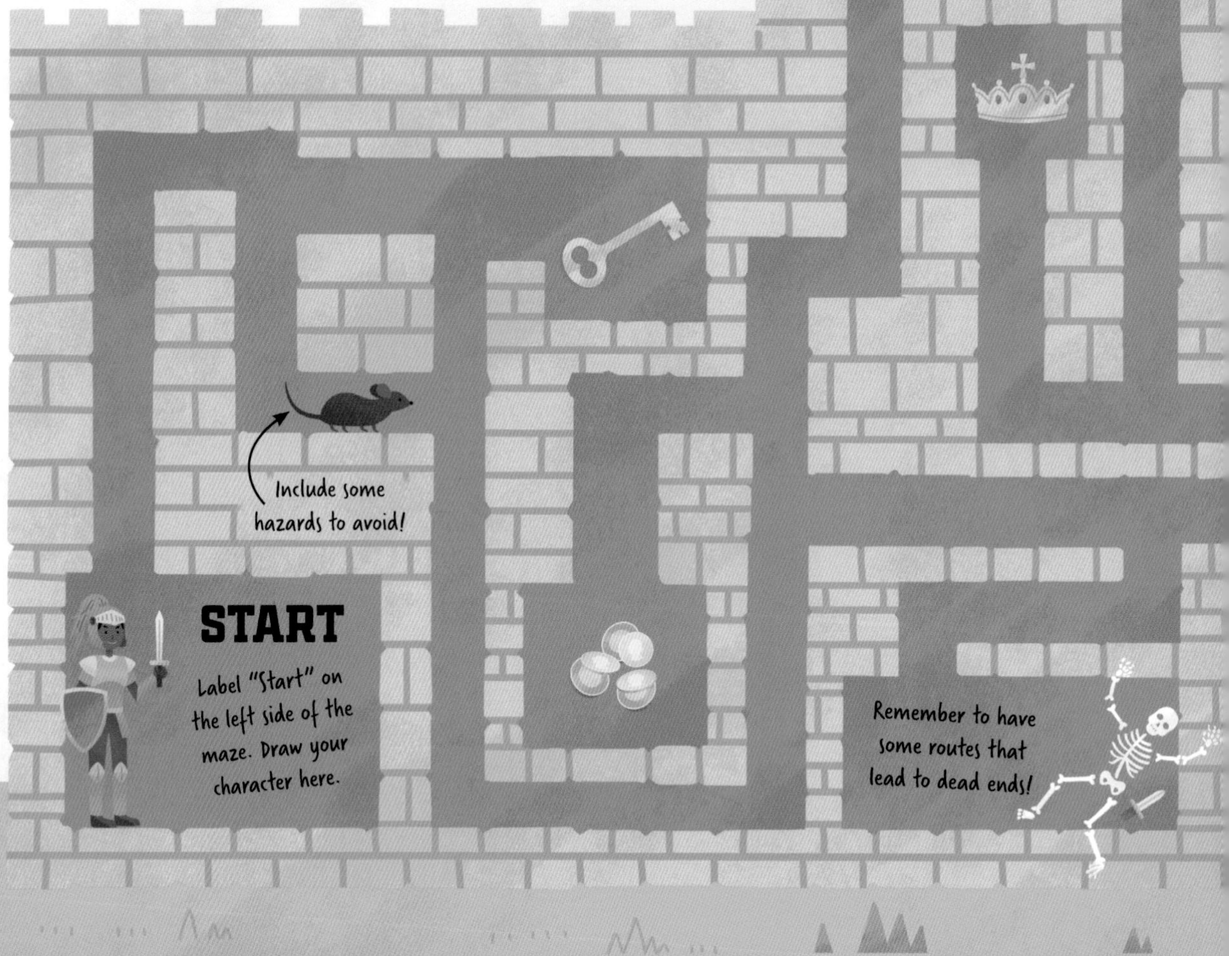

For an extra challenge, you could add keys, gold coins, or a crown to collect along the way. All of them must be gathered before reaching the finish.

Include some hazards to avoid!

START

Label "Start" on the left side of the maze. Draw your character here.

Remember to have some routes that lead to dead ends!

FINISH

Mark "Finish" in the center or on the right side of the maze.

Be sure that there is one winding path that leads you from start to finish.

Many mazes

Try different styles of mazes. Draw a picture using natural paths, or create a more traditional straight-line labyrinth.

WORD SEARCH

Hide words in plain sight! Create your own word search full of **hidden vacation words.** Then pass it to an eagle-eyed contestant. Can they find them all?

You will need
• Paper
• Ruler
• Pen

How to make and play

1 Using your ruler and pen, draw a 10x10 grid on your paper.

2 Choose 10 vacation words. Write them in a list near the grid.

3 Now write each word in the grid, placing one letter only in each box. Words can go across, down, or diagonally. Space out the words around the grid.

Overlap some words with the same letters if you like!

I			
C			
E			
C	R	A	B
R			
E			
A			
M			

T	A	T	D	H	X	F	T	S	K
L	H	O	S	I	W	S	E	A	S
Y	X	W	K	C	B	V	R	J	U
P	C	E	T	E	T	J	H	T	N
I	F	L	R	C	R	A	B	B	D
C	D	U	X	R	T	N	E	N	F
N	K	M	Z	E	W	J	A	M	W
I	S	L	C	A	T	S	C	T	Y
C	Z	W	H	M	D	N	H	A	T
H	S	H	O	V	E	L	T	R	S

ice cream   sea   hat   sand   towel

~~crab~~   beach   shovel   sun   picnic

4 Fill all the remaining boxes in the grid with random letters. These will hide where your words are!

5 Give your word search to a family member or friend. Can they find all 10 hidden words?

WORD CLUES

In this game, the words aren't there at all! Give clues for a **clever contender** to figure out the missing words.

You will need
- Paper
- Pen

How to make and play

1 Think of a list of 10 words related to your vacation. Write them on a piece of paper.

2 On a separate piece of paper, draw a series of dashes, with one dash for each letter in the first word on your list. For example, if your word is "mountain," you would draw eight dashes.

Example:

— — — — — — — —

3 Next to the dashes, write a clue about your word, without saying what it is. For example, for "mountain" you could write, "People climb to the top of this."

4 Repeat steps 2 and 3 for each of the words on your list.

5 Hand this paper over to a friend or family member. Keep the list of words to yourself!

6 Ask your friend or family member to fill in the boxes, using your clues to help. Can they get them all right?

Instead of descriptive clues, you could draw a picture of the item.

Or, go with a list of animals you might see on your vacation, and use the sound they make as their clues!

THE CHALLENGER

Fold your way to fun! Using the Japanese art of origami, fold a paper device to **set silly challenges** for a friend. Who **dares to take it on**?

How to make

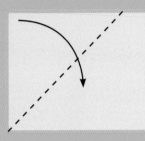

1 Fold the top left corner of your paper down to the bottom edge, to create a diagonal crease.

2 Cut off the strip of paper to the side, so just the triangle shape remains.

3 Unfold the paper. Fold the top right corner down to the bottom left corner. Crease and unfold.

4 Fold each corner in to the center. Crease well.

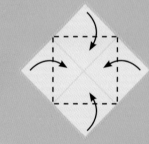

5 Turn the paper over. Fold the corners in to the center. Crease well.

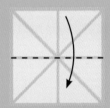

6 Fold the top edge down to the bottom edge to create a horizontal crease, then unfold.

7 Fold the left edge across to the right edge to create a vertical crease, then unfold.

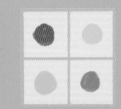

8 Turn the paper over. Draw a large spot in a different color on each square, as shown.

Try and think of four colors with different numbers of letters in their names.

9 Turn the paper back over and write the numbers 1 to 8 on the triangles, as shown.

10 Lift one of the flaps. Write a challenge on the left triangle, such as, "Do 10 push-ups." Write a different challenge on the right triangle, such as, "Pat your head and rub your tummy."

11 Repeat step 10 for each of the remaining three flaps, writing a different challenge in each half, until you have eight different challenges written out. Fold all the flaps down again.

12 Slide your thumb and index finger from each hand under the square flaps on the reverse. Pinch all the points toward the center. Your challenger is now ready—who will you challenge first?

How to play

1 Ask a friend to choose a color from the top. Move the challenger back and forth for each letter of the color they chose, such as three times for R-E-D.

2 Now ask your friend to choose a number from the ones showing. Move the challenger back and forth that number of times.

3 Ask your friend to choose a number from the numbers showing now. Move the challenger back and forth that number of times again.

4 Ask your friend to choose one last number. Open the flap and read the challenge below that number. Challenge your friend to do the task there and then!

SHOUT YOUR NAME AS LOUD AS YOU CAN!

EAT SOMETHING WITHOUT USING YOUR HANDS!

TRY TO TOUCH YOUR NOSE WITH YOUR TONGUE!

FILL IN THE GAPS

Make up a **random story** together by filling in blanks with funny words. The catch is that one of you **doesn't know what's going on**!

You will need
- Paper
- Pencil

How to make and play

1 Write a story on your piece of paper. Draw lines to leave gaps for some words, labeling them just as adjective, noun, verb, or another type of word that fits.

2 Don't show the story to your partner! Ask them to give you a word for each of the gaps, one at a time. For example, if you labeled the first gap "noun," ask for a noun. If they say "dragon," write in "dragon" on the first line.

3 Continue asking your partner for the remaining missing words in your story, writing them in as you go.

4 Now read your story out loud! How ridiculous is it?

We had the most _**disgusting**_ (adjective) vacation ever!

First, we went _**running**_ (verb) up a _**bridge**_ (noun).

**Dad** (person's name) fell down! "_**Ouch**_!" (funny noise)

he shouted. We stopped for a picnic and ate lots of

_____ (food) and drank _____ (drink).

After that we all felt _____ (adjective). We

_____ (verb) the rest of the way home. The next

day we took a _____ (noun) out on the water.

The day after that, we went _____ (verb) with

some new friends. By the end of the vacation, we were

_____ (adjective)!

Think of more specific gaps you could leave in your story. What about 'funny noise' or 'food'?

MIX-AND-MATCH MONSTERS

It's time to **draw together**! Make a mix-and-match masterpiece by each drawing a section of a monster. What **new beast** will you create?

How to make and play

Leave little lines poking out where the neck is so the next player can line up the body.

You will need
• Paper
• Felt-tip pens

1 Fold your paper equally into three. Crease then unfold. The first person draws a head in the top third of the paper. They fold it over backward so no one can see what they've drawn.

2 The next person draws the middle section of a monster, down to the top of the legs. This could include arms, a funny shirt, and accessories. They fold it backward to hide their drawing, leaving only the lines at the bottom of the body showing.

3 The last person draws legs, flippers, or anything else they can think of to finish the monster.

4 Unfold the paper to reveal your mix-and-match monster!

Mega-monster!

If you've got lots of people to play with, make a mega-monster! Find an extra-long sheet of paper or tape some pieces together. Have each person add a section, then fold it back. Keep going until everyone has had a turn. Unfold the paper to see what you've created together!

The first person draws the head.

Everyone else draws a middle section.

The last person draws the feet.

Creature creation

You can play this game with any type of character drawing. Instead of monsters, try people, animals, or superheroes.

MIXED-UP MONSTERS!

PLAY WITH NUMBERS

Add excitement to math with these **playful number games**. Count, guess, calculate, and solve your way through. Who can you **count on** to find the answers?

You will need
- Paper
- Felt-tip pens
- Pencil
- Eraser

GUESS-TIMATE

Draw a circle on your piece of paper. Now draw objects in the circle, such as stars or hearts. Keep count of the number of objects that you draw, but don't let anyone know the final count! Ask each player to guess how many objects are in the circle by looking but not counting. Who can guess closest to the actual number? Now let someone else have a turn drawing the items, and play again!

You could draw a few different types of objects and have players guess how many there are of each one!

NUMBER SQUARES

Draw a 3x3 grid on your paper. Using only the digits 1 to 7, can you make each row and column add up to the number 10?

You could also erase some of the numbers in your grid after you've completed it and hand it to another player to complete. Can they fill in the blanks?

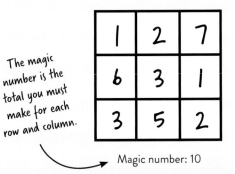

The magic number is the total you must make for each row and column.

Magic number: 10

Magic number: 10

To make the game harder, don't use a number more than once in any row or column. Try the game with bigger grids and different magic numbers, too!

RIDDLE ME THIS

Can you solve these tricky problems? Figure them out on your paper. Then try making up some number riddles for your friends and family! Make sure you know the answers, too.

WHEN MILO WAS 6 YEARS OLD, HIS OLDER BROTHER EZRA WAS TWICE HIS AGE.

MILO IS 20 NOW.

HOW OLD IS EZRA?

I AM A THREE-DIGIT NUMBER. MY FIRST DIGIT FALLS BETWEEN 3 AND 5.

MY SECOND DIGIT IS TWO TIMES BIGGER THAN MY FIRST DIGIT.

MY THIRD DIGIT IS FIVE LESS THAN MY SECOND DIGIT. WHAT NUMBER AM I?

PAPER BOAT RACES

Make boats that really **float** from just a **piece of paper**. Then set them sailing and see whose boat can reach the finish line the **fastest**!

You will need

- Letter-sized paper
- Cocktail picks (optional)

How to make and play

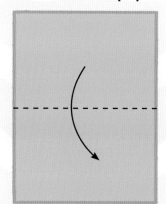

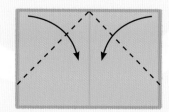

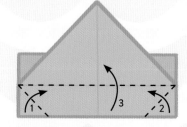

1 Lay the paper flat on the table, short side at the bottom. Fold the top edge down to the bottom.

2 Fold the right edge to the left edge. Crease, then unfold.

3 Fold both top corners in towards the central crease.

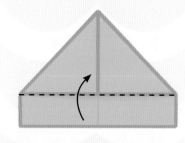

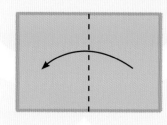

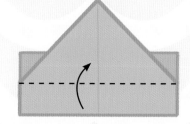

4 Fold the top layer of the horizontal strip up, as shown.

5 Turn over. Fold the remaining layer up, as shown, then unfold.

6 Fold the bottom left corner up to the crease line you just made. Repeat on the right, then fold the whole strip up.

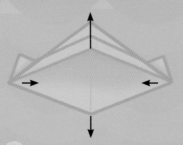

Open

7 Slide your finger into the gap at the bottom to open it up. Turn the opening towards you.

8 Pull the opening apart, until the paper flattens along the crease you made earlier.

9 Rotate your paper so it looks like this. Tuck the front flap into the flap beneath it. Turn over and repeat on the reverse.

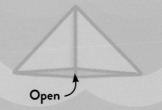

Open

10 Fold up the bottom point of the upper layer as shown. Turn the paper over and repeat on the other side.

11 Slide your finger into the gap at the bottom to open it up. Turn the opening toward you.

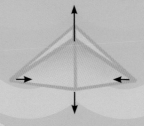

12 Continue to open it up until the paper flattens, as you did in step 8.

Pull   **Pull**

13 Gently pull the top two points apart, as shown.

Pull   **Pull**

14 Keep pulling until you get a boat shape. Turn up the edges and shape as needed.

Wrap a piece of paper around a cocktail pick to make a flag.

READY, STEADY, GO!

Release your boats and see whose can reach the finish line first.

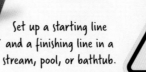

Use different colored pieces of paper so you know whose boat is whose, or write your names on them.

Set up a starting line and a finishing line in a stream, pool, or bathtub.

WARNING
Always have an adult around when playing near the water!

Labels on the map:

bird
red leaves
red berries
red berries
flowers
yellow leaves
flowers
orange leaves
pine cone
red berries
yellow leaves
yellow leaves
rabbit
orange leaves
bird

CARD AND BOARD GAMES

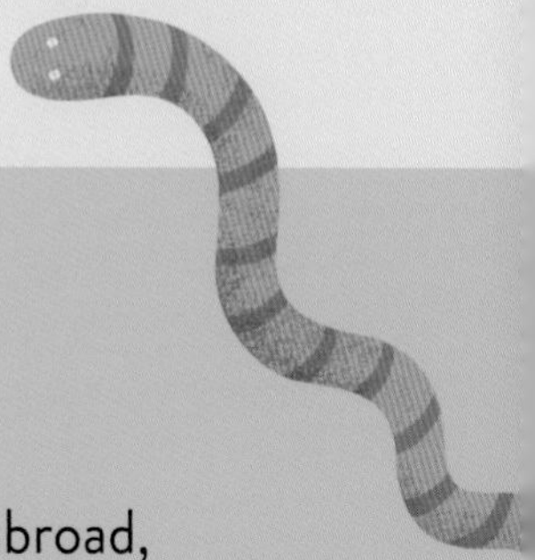

Whether you're on a staycation or traveling abroad, board and card games are the perfect way to **pass the time** or just **have a good time**. Use simple supplies that you can find around you to create your own games: some classic, some extra challenging, and some super personalized! Settle in, roll the dice, and **get gaming**!

SIR SCARE-A-LOT

STRENGTH	33
SCARINESS	92
BRAVERY	81
RATING	69

CLASSIC FUN

Go **back to basics** with a classic board game. Come up with a theme and decorate your board to match. Then **challenge** some family or friends to a game!

How to make

1 Decide on your theme and the quest.

2 On one sheet of paper, draw a series of squares or stepping stones.

3 Decorate the board to match your theme. If it's a creepy castle, draw turrets and cobwebs. If it's outer space, add stars and planets!

4 Write extra instructions, such as "Miss a turn" or "Move forward 2 spaces," on some of the squares. Space these apart along the path. Tie them into your theme for extra fun!

5 On another piece of paper, trace the dice template on page 144. Write the numbers 1 to 6 on the different squares. Cut out, fold, and glue to create a cube.

You will need
- Paper
- Felt-tip pens
- Objects to use as tokens, such as different colored buttons, coins, stones, or small toy figures

Travel to the green portal.

You speed up to avoid asteroids! Move forward 3 spaces.

You get caught in a meteor shower. Go back 2 spaces.

Whoosh to the blue portal.

START

Label the start and finish.

FINISH

You spot Saturn. Go forward 2 spaces.

Engine failure! Move back 1 space.

Decorate your game board.

Your radio fails. Miss a turn.

The rocket needs repairing. Move back 1 space.

You get a blast of rocket power. Roll again.

Label your special squares!

How to play

1 Choose a token per player. Place these items on the start space.

2 The youngest player goes first. On a player's turn, they roll the dice, then move their token that many spaces forward. If they land on a special square, they must follow the instructions.

3 Each player rolls the dice and moves in turn.

4 The first player to reach the finish wins!

Special squares

Think about how your special squares match your theme. For a creepy castle for example, you could say:

• You're stuck in a cobweb. Miss a turn.
• A knight is chasing you. Run forward 3 squares.
• You rescue a cat from the tower. Roll again.

For a space-themed game like this one, you could add portals to jump around the board. If you land on one portal, it could tell you to transport to another.

79

TRAVEL CARDS

Make your own cards to play these well-known games. Then find a worthy opponent and put your reflexes and minds to the test. **Snap to it**!

How to make

1 Lay one sheet of cardstock on a flat surface, long side facing you. Fold it in half, bringing the top to the bottom. Crease, then open it out again.

2 Fold the right edge to the left edge.

3 Fold the right edge to the left edge again.

4 Unfold the whole sheet. Cut along the creased lines. You should now have eight smaller cards.

5 Draw a different travel picture on each of the eight cards. These could be places that you've visited or famous landmarks that you'd like to see.

6 Repeat steps 1 to 5 using another piece of cardstock. Draw the same pictures on this set, so that you have 16 cards in total with matching pairs of eight pictures.

These are your playing cards!

For more challenging games, repeat these steps to make even more cards!

You will need
- 2 sheets of letter-sized cardstock
- Scissors
- Felt-tip pens

SNAP!

How to play

1 Shuffle the cards all together.

2 Deal the cards evenly between two players, pictures face down.

3 At the same time, both players flip the top card over from their pile. If the pictures on the cards are the same, yell "Snap!" The first person to shout this collects all the flipped cards and puts them at the bottom of their pile. If the cards do not match, continue flipping the top cards together until they do.

4 The game ends when one person collects all the cards.

MEMORY

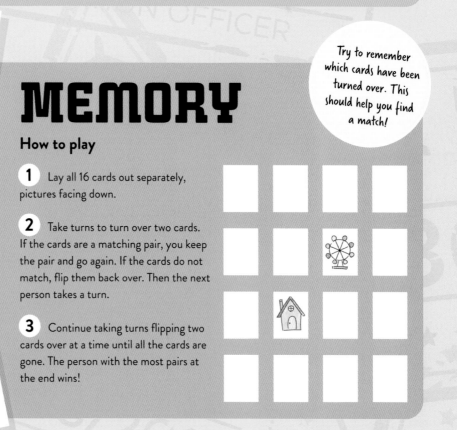

Try to remember which cards have been turned over. This should help you find a match!

How to play

1 Lay all 16 cards out separately, pictures facing down.

2 Take turns to turn over two cards. If the cards are a matching pair, you keep the pair and go again. If the cards do not match, flip them back over. Then the next person takes a turn.

3 Continue taking turns flipping two cards over at a time until all the cards are gone. The person with the most pairs at the end wins!

SNAKES AND LADDERS

Start with a grid, then let your imagination **run wild**! Will you try the traditional snakes and ladders, or **invent your own**? Prepare to travel up and down in this rollercoaster of a game.

You will need

- Letter-sized paper
- Scissors
- Ruler
- Pencil
- Felt-tip pens
- Glue
- Objects to use as tokens, such as different colored buttons, coins, stones, or small toy figures

100	99	98	97	96	95	94	93	92	91
81	82	83	84	85	86	87	88	89	90
80	79	78	77	76	75	74	73	72	71
61	62	63	64	65	66	67	68	69	70
60	59	58	57	56	55	54	53	52	51
41	42	43	44	45	46	47	48	49	50
40	39	38	37	36	35	34	33	32	31
21	22	23	24	25	26	27	28	29	30
20	19	18	17	16	15	14	13	12	11
1	2	3	4	5	6	7	8	9	10

How to make

1. Lay the paper flat, short side at the bottom. Fold the top right corner to the left edge.

2. Cut along the bottom line as shown. Open the triangle. You should now have a square.

3. Use your ruler to make marks every 2.1 cm across the page.

4. Draw straight lines down with your ruler and pencil at each of these marks. You should end up with 10 columns.

5. Rotate the paper and repeat steps 3 and 4. You should now have a grid of 100 squares.

6. Write number 1 in the bottom left corner. Then continue numbering each square from 1 to 100, zigzagging up the grid. Square 100 should end up in the top left.

7. Draw snakes and ladders on your board! Place them wherever you like, but space them apart. For snakes, draw a head higher than the tail, so when you play you slide down the snake from head to tail.

Make your dice

Trace the dice template on page 144. Write the numbers 1 to 6 on the different squares. Cut out, fold, and glue to create a cube.

100 FINISH	99	98	97	96	95	94			
81	82	83	84	85	86	8			
80	79	78	77	76	75	74			
61	62	63	64	65	66	67	68	69	70
60	59	58	57	56	55	54	53	52	51
41	42	43	44	45	46	47	48	49	50
40	39	38	37	36	35	34	33	32	31
21	22	23	24	25	26	27	28	29	30
20	19	18	17	16	15	14	13	12	11
1 START	2	3	4	5				9	10

Invent your own

The key to snakes and ladders is having objects that take you up the board, and others that slide you down. Think about your own version. What could you use instead of ladders and snakes? Slides rather than snakes? Or you could make a space-themed board and have rockets to go up and comets to go down. What can you think up?

Make sure to put the heads, tails, and ladder tops and bottoms clearly within squares, so you know where they start and end.

How to play

1 Choose a token per player. Place these items on the start square.

2 Roll the dice to decide who goes first. The highest roll starts the game.

3 On a player's turn, they roll the dice, then move their token that many spaces forward.

4 If they land at the bottom of a ladder, they climb to the space at the top. But if they land on a snake's head, they must slide down to its tail!

5 Each player rolls the dice and moves in turn.

6 The first player to reach the finish wins!

ESCAPE ROOM

An escape room is a game where you must solve a series of puzzles to—you guessed it—**escape a room**! Create your own mysterious escape room board game, and then find a friend or family member **up for the challenge**. Can they escape?

You will need
- Paper
- Felt-tip pens

How to make and play

Step 1: Choose your setting
An escape room can be any kind of room or building you can imagine. You could be a prisoner trapped in a dungeon or a detective trying to solve a crime in a closed room. You could be a spy in a high-tech facility or an explorer searching for lost treasure. Plan your place, and come up with a story for it, too.

Step 2: Draw the room
On a sheet of paper, draw the outline of your room or rooms. Then divide it into smaller sections that you need to work through to get from the start to the finish. Draw the finish, whether that's the item you need to retrieve or the door out!

Step 3: Write your riddles
Write one riddle in each section. The player must solve the riddles to pass. These could be math problems, word riddles, code breakers, or more. Try the ideas on the facing page to get you started.

Step 4: Challenge a friend
Now find a friend to take on the challenge. Ask them to place their fingers at the start. Can they solve the first riddle? If so, they can pass on to the next. Check their answers are correct before you let them through. Will they make a clean break and escape your game?

START

1. Open the padlock to unlock the door. What is the next number in the sequence?

| 2 | 4 | 8 | 16 | 32 | |

2. There's a secret passageway behind these stones! Find the missing puzzle piece to complete the picture and find the way out.

A   B   C   D

3. I'm tall when I'm young and short when I'm old. What am I? Find me in this room to move on.

4. Read this article, then solve the code for the door.

_ _ _ _ _ _ _ _ _

OLD TOMB DISCOVERED!

Archaeologists have discovered an untouched tomb more than 30 feet (9 meters) underground. So far, 27 sarcophagi have been uncovered. The question is, what other secrets will they find in this 2,500-year-old sacred site?

YOU'VE ESCAPED!

EXIT

85

EXPLORER ESCAPADES

This game uses a spinner instead of a dice to move **north, south, east, or west**. Travel around the board to explore a new place and **reach your destination**. What will you see along your travels?

You will need
- Letter-sized paper
- Ruler
- Sharp pencil
- Felt-tip pens
- Large mug or cup
- Cardstock
- Scissors
- Objects to use as tokens, such as different colored buttons, coins, stones, or small toy figures

How to make

1 With the paper short side down, fold the right edge to the left. Crease. Fold the right edge to the left again. Crease, then unfold both folds.

2 Now fold the paper in half from top to bottom. Crease. Fold in half from top to bottom again. Crease. Open up the last fold you made.

3 Fold the top and bottom in to the center line. Crease. Unfold the entire paper and smooth it out. You should now have a paper divided into 32 squares.

4 Use a ruler and pencil to draw lines over the top of the creases to make the game squares clear.

5 Mark a start square two squares down and two squares in from the top right. Mark a finish square three squares up and two squares in from the bottom left.

6 Now have fun marking up some special squares! Decide the location that you're exploring and the obstacles that might get in your way. For example, for a jungle game, you could say, "It's so hot! Miss a turn while you stop to rest."

Make the spinner

To make the spinner, trace around a mug or cup to draw a circle on the cardstock. Cut out this circle. Using your ruler, draw two lines diagonally across the middle to divide the circle into four quarters. Mark each quarter North, East, South, or West, as shown.

Poke the pointed end of the pencil through the center of the spinner.

1 How to play

Place your tokens on the start square. The youngest player goes first. They spin the spinner and move one square in the direction it lands on.

Mark North, East, South, and West on your board so you know which way to go.

You hear tropical birds up ahead. Move west 2 spaces to investigate.

N
▲
W ◄ **START** ► E
▼
S

You seem to be lost. Miss a turn to check the map.

2

Take turns to spin and move around the board, following any instructions on special squares. If a spin takes you off the board, stay where you are and spin again.

You found a short cut! Spin again.

There's a snake in the trees! Run away 2 spaces south.

3

The first player to reach the finish wins!

FINISH

Camp for the night. Miss a turn.

Stop to watch the sloths. Miss a turn.

4

If the game is going on without anyone reaching the finish, set a time limit. When the time runs out, the player nearest to the finish wins.

JUMBO DOMINOES

Make a domino **matching game** using card, sticks, or stones.
Decorate your dominoes with vacation pictures, then **get playing!**

You will need
- 3 sheets of letter-sized cardstock
- Scissors
- Felt-tip pens
- Ruler

How to make

1 Lay one sheet of cardstock on a flat surface, long side facing you. Fold it in half, bringing the top to the bottom.

2 Fold the right edge to the left edge.

3 Fold the right edge to the left edge again.

4 Unfold the whole sheet. Cut along the creased lines. You should now have eight smaller cards.

5 Repeat steps 1 to 4 using two more pieces of cardstock. You should now have 24 smaller cards in total.

6 Using a pen and ruler, draw a line across the center of each card.

7 Decide on six different travel pictures you'd like on your cards. These could be a palm tree, a sandcastle, an airplane, a flamingo pool float, or anything else you can think of! Draw each picture on one of the eight domino halves. Mix and match so you have different combinations on each card.

How to play

1 Shuffle the cards. Deal four cards to each person. Place the rest of the dominoes in a pile face down on the table.

2 Turn over the top card of the pile and place it in the center of the table.

3 The oldest player goes first. They lay a card down to match the picture on either end of the domino on the table using one of the dominoes in their hand. If they can't make a match, they draw from the pile. If there is still no match, they keep the new card and their turn ends.

4 Players take turns playing dominoes, matching to either open end of the chain on the table (not to pictures in the middle).

5 The first player to play all the dominoes in their hand wins!

Sticks and stones

Instead of using cardstock, you could collect objects from your vacation to make your dominoes, such as ice pop sticks or stones from outside. Find 24 items. Paint the sticks or stones in bright colors and leave to dry. Then with a permanent marker, draw a line across the center of each one. Write the numbers 1 to 6 on the dominoes, writing each number in eight different halves.

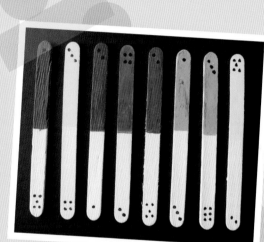

Turn the dominoes if they start going off the table!

You could also include a couple of stones that you leave blank. These are wildcards and can match with any number!

YOUR VACATION GAME

This is YOUR vacation game. Turn your trip into a **game of its own** with this game board based on your getaway and familiar objects to move you along. It's **personalized fun!**

You will need
- Paper
- Felt-tip pens
- Cardstock
- Scissors
- Adhesive putty or tape

bird

red leaves

flowers

yellow leaves

orange leaves

red berries

yellow leaves

pine cone

rabbit

Plan your route

First things first. Decide on which part of your vacation you'll use as the game. Will it be the journey from your home to the destination? Or, will your game be based around your vacation itself? If you're at a campsite by the beach, you could draw the tent and the path you take to the beach as a winding game path with things you might spot along the way.

START

FINISH

bird

yellow leaves

red leaves

orange leaves

flowers

red leaves

red berries

flowers

red berries

orange leaves

bird

flowers

yellow leaves

flowers

yellow leaves

orange leaves

bird

How to make

1 On your sheet of paper, draw the start and finish of your game. Then draw a route in between. This could be the road to your vacation or a path through the woods by your cabin.

2 Draw objects that you might see repeated along the route. For the journey board, you could add different colored cars, a train, and a bus stop. For the winding woods, add birds, squirrels, different colored leaves, and more.

3 To make your playing pieces, draw small versions of you and the other players on the piece of cardstock. Cut them out. Place a small amount of adhesive putty or tape on the back.

How to play

1 To play the game, stick all the players to the start. Look carefully as you journey along in real life. Every time a player spots an object on the board, they can move their piece forward to the next instance of that object.

2 The first player to reach the finish wins!

WEAVING CHECKERS

No checkers set in your vacation home? No problem! You can **make one** with cardstock and objects you find on vacation. Then use **cunning, skill, and strategy** to beat your opponent in a game.

How to make

1 Lay the paper down, long edge at the bottom. Fold the right edge to the left edge, then fold the top edge to the bottom edge. Fold the top edge to the bottom edge again. Finally, fold the top edge to the bottom edge one more time, then unfold. Your paper should look like the above image.

2 Fold the right edge to the left edge again. Cut along each crease starting at the fold on the right edge and stopping 2.5 cm from the left edge. Open up the paper. You should end up with seven horizontal slits in your page, as above.

3 Lay another piece of cardstock flat, long edge at the bottom. Fold the top edge to the bottom edge. Fold the top edge to the bottom edge again. Finally, fold the top edge to the bottom edge one more time, then unfold the whole sheet.

4 Cut along the creases completely so that you have eight long strips of paper.

5 Weave one strip through the slits in the first piece of cardstock. Go in and out of the slits, as shown. Repeat with each strip, alternating whether you start weaving over or under to create a checked effect.

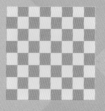

6 Push all the strips together toward the left end to create even squares. Glue all the ends down to secure in place, then trim the edges of the board so you end up with a checked 8x8 square, as above.

Prepare your pieces:

Divide your shells or stones into two equal piles of 16. Paint one group of 16 in one color, and the other group of 16 in another color. Leave to dry.

If you don't have paint with you on vacation, one player could use 16 shells and the other player could use 16 stones. Or, cut out circles of different colored cardstock!

King me!

Capture!

Jump!

How to play

1 Choose a piece color for each player. Position the board so that the darker of the square colors is in the bottom left closest to you.

2 Each player places 12 of their playing pieces on the darker squares of the first three rows of the board facing them. Keep the other four pieces aside.

3 The lighter playing pieces go first. Pieces can only move forward diagonally, one square at a time. You cannot move onto a space where you already have a piece.

4 If there is an opponent's piece in your way, you can jump over it to an empty space. This captures the piece. Place it in your pile.

5 When one of your playing pieces reaches the far end of the board, it becomes a king. Pile a second playing piece on top to show its special status. Use adhesive putty if you need to! It can now move both forward and backward diagonally around the board. If a king is jumped, the player who captured it takes both pieces.

6 Take turns to move a piece.

7 The aim of the game is to capture all of your opponent's pieces, or block all of their moves.

WHO COULD IT BE?

You will need
• 5 sheets of letter-sized cardstock
• Ruler
• Pencil
• Scissors
• Felt-tip pens
• Glue stick

Laugh together making and playing this **personalized** game. Make the game boards using **real friends and family**, and then ask simple questions to deduce who the mystery person could be!

How to make

Draw one more rectangle at the bottom of the page. Leave this one blank.

1   Using your ruler and pencil, draw 16 rectangles spaced slightly apart in a 4x4 grid on one sheet of cardstock, as shown. Light-colored card is best for this.

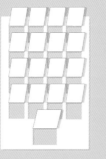

2   Ask an adult to carefully cut out the sides and bottom of each rectangle, leaving the top uncut. Fold each rectangle up along the top edge.

You could also glue on a photo of each person if you've got these around and have permission!

3   Using colored felt-tip pens, draw a different family member, friend, or even pet on each of the top 16 folded-up rectangles. Write their name below their picture.

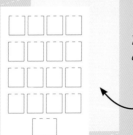

You could use a different color cardstock if you like.

4   Fold all the pictures down. Place the sheet on one other piece of cardstock, lining up the edges. Double check that the flaps flip up to reveal a person the right way around, then carefully glue the top card down, making sure not to glue any of the flaps.

5   Lift up all the flaps so the board is ready for the start of the game. Repeat steps 1 to 4 to create a second game board. Use the same characters, but put them in different positions on the board.

6   Cut 16 rectangles out of the last piece of cardstock. Draw the 16 characters and write their names on each of these. This is your deck. Place it upside down on the table.

ARE THEY RELATED TO ME?

DO THEY WEAR GLASSES?

DO THEY HAVE A MUSTACHE?

ARE THEY OLDER THAN 10?

Mohammed

Atlas

Grandad

Emily   Gran   Uncle Steve   Daisy

Oliver   Aunty Jean   Grandad

Mia   Jessica   Jack   Mom

Dad   Mohammed   Atlas   Eden

Use adhesive putty to help keep your card in place. →

Maya

How to play

1 Each player places a game board in front of them with all characters standing up.

2 Each player takes one card from the deck. Keep this mystery character hidden from the other player by placing it in your bottom window. Fold down the matching character on your board.

3 Take turns to ask a yes or no question to the other player to try to deduce their mystery character.

4 Each time the other person answers, fold down any people on your board who do NOT match the answer. For example, if you asked, "Does this person wear glasses?" and your opponent answered "Yes," fold down any character who ISN'T wearing glasses. This should leave up only the people who are. After you've folded down your characters, the other person goes. Keep taking turns to ask questions until you can guess who it might be.

5 When you think you know your opponent's mystery character, on your turn, make a guess! If you guess incorrectly, continue with the game. The first person to guess the correct mystery person wins. Just for fun, you could carry on guessing until both characters are revealed.

WHO could it be?

IS YOUR PERSON A BOY?

DO THEY HAVE CURLY HAIR?

ARE THEIR EYES BROWN?

DO THEY HAVE A HAT?

Mom

Dad

95

TOP SCORE

This is a game for everyone! Choose your favorite category, make your own set of cards, and set some scores. Then play the cards **head to head**... Who will come out **on top**?

You will need

- 3 sheets of letter-sized cardstock
- Scissors
- Ruler
- Pencil
- Felt-tip pens

CHEETAH

These are your three categories.

SIZE	60
SPECIAL SKILLS	95
FEAR FACTOR	80
RATING	78

How to make

1 Lay one sheet of cardstock on a flat surface, long side facing you. Fold it in half, bringing the top to the bottom.

2 Fold the right edge to the left edge. Fold the right edge to the left edge again.

3 Unfold the whole sheet. Cut along the creased lines. You should now have eight smaller cards.

4 Repeat steps 1 to 3 using the two other pieces of cardstock. You should now have 24 cards in total.

5 Choose a theme for your cards, such as Made-up Monsters, Mighty Superheroes, or Awesome Animals of the World! Then choose three categories for your cards.

6 Using your ruler and pencil, draw a horizontal line halfway down the card. Draw four more lines below it.

7 In the top half of the card, draw a creature or character for your theme, such as a cheetah for Animals, a furry made-up monster for Monsters, or a favorite superhero. Write their name at the top of the card.

8 On the lines below, write the three category names. Give your character a score for each category out of 100. Finally, give an overall rating at the bottom. This is usually an average score, so add together the scores of the different categories, then divide by three.

9 Repeat steps 6 to 8 for each of the cards, drawing a different character for each one. You should end up with a deck of 24 different characters within your overall theme.

MR. TENTACULAR

STRENGTH	75
SCARINESS	78
BRAVERY	65
RATING	73

SIR SCARE-A-LOT

STRENGTH	33
SCARINESS	92
BRAVERY	81
RATING	69

FLUFFY BOB

STRENGTH	40
SCARINESS	45
BRAVERY	87
RATING	57

How to play

1 Shuffle all the cards together. Then deal them out evenly among the players, pictures face down.

2 Each player picks up their top card only, looking at the picture side without sharing it with the other players.

3 The player to the left of the dealer chooses a category from their card. They read out the category name and its score, such as "Special Skills 95."

4 Going in a clockwise direction, the remaining players read the score of the same category from the card in their hand. The person with the highest score wins all the cards from the round. They place them at the bottom of their pile.

5 The person who wins the cards calls out the category for the next card.

6 Continue playing until one player has all the cards in the deck. They are the winner!

Note:
If there is a tie for the top score, choose a different category and try again.

SPECIAL SKILLS 45!

I WIN THIS ONE!

95!

OUTDOOR GAMES

Go wild with your imagination and invent games to play, using the **great outdoors** as your guide. Whether you're at the beach, in the woods, or in the garden, you can find sticks, sand, trees, and stones that will provide hours of entertainment, if you use them wisely... So step outside, and **start playing**!

COURSE OF OBSTACLES

Build your own **obstacle course** and set extra **challenges,** too. Climb, crawl, and jump through the barriers to make your way to the **finish line**!

Balance beam

Use a flat piece of wood, an old log, or a fallen branch. Tiptoe across without falling off!

Hula hoop

Hang a hula hoop from a tree or have someone hold it up for you. Can you go through without touching the edges? For an extra challenge, tie bells to the top and try not to make them ring!

Laser maze

Weave string back and forth, attaching it to trees or posts. Mix it up so some pieces are angled upward and others are angled downward. Then crawl and climb through the gaps— see if you can clear the maze without touching the string!

Hurdles

Push sticks into the ground. Tie string from stick to stick. Or, lay long sticks horizontally on the ground. Then hop, skip, and jump your way across!

Commando crawl

Place two or four garden chairs back to back, slightly apart. Drape a blanket over the chairs. Use hair ties, clothes pins, or string to secure the blanket to the chair backs. Now crawl, roll, or slither underneath!

Do the dodge

Set up a line of obstacles using bottles, buckets, or anything else you have on hand. Weave your way through! Dribble a ball around the obstacles for an extra challenge.

THE FLOOR IS LAVA

Set up stepping stones made of big rocks, pieces of wood, buckets, blankets, or anything you can find that's safe and steady to step on. Make your way across these, but remember—the ground is hot lava, so don't fall in!

Turn your obstacle course into a daring game of balance and skill.

Extra life

Place some objects in the "lava" area around the course, such as a shovel, a plant pot, or a rock. When you touch these special objects, you earn an extra life. Start with three lives and lose a life every time you touch the "lava." Can you make it across before you lose all your lives?

STICK GAMES

When you're **outside**, you can use what's **around you** to make and play fun games—including the **simple stick**!

RACING STICKS

How to play

1   Each player chooses a special stick from the ground. Try to find sticks with a distinguishing feature, such as a leaf sticking out or a pointy end, so that you can tell them apart.

2   Find a bridge over a stream or river. Check which way the water is flowing. Stand on the side of the bridge where the water flows underneath.

3   On the count of three, drop your sticks into the water.

4   Run to the other side of the bridge, where the water flows out. Look down. Whose stick comes out first?

5   If you can't find a bridge, set starting and finishing lines along a flowing stream instead using sticks as markers.

PICK-UP STICKS

STICK AT IT!

How to play

1 Gather at least 10 short sticks.

2 Hold all the sticks in your hands, just above the ground. Then drop them! Push them into a small pile if needed.

3 Take turns to remove one stick from the pile without making the others move. If you can remove the stick without shifting the others, you keep it and have another go. If the other sticks move, your turn ends. Whoever has the most sticks when the pile is gone wins!

Stick trick
You could keep one special "helper" stick aside to use to lift the others if needed.

STICK TALES

How to play

1 Find a nice solid stick. Wrap string around it and secure with a knot at each end.

2 When you go on a nature walk with your family, pick up natural items that mean something to you. You could pick up a leaf from the spot where you had a picnic or a feather near where you spotted beautiful birds. Tuck the items into the string on your stick.

3 Back at home, share the story of your nature adventure, using each item on the stick as your guide.

TREASURE QUEST

Arrr! Channel your **inner pirate** and hide some treasure for others to find. **Make a map** to help them with their quest!

Wait a few minutes for the water to turn dark brown.

You will need
- Teabag
- Bowl of warm water
- Spoon
- Dish cloth
- Letter-sized paper
- Sponge
- Something to hide as treasure (such as a toy or chocolate coins)
- Felt-tip pens
- Ribbon

1 Place the teabag in the bowl of warm water. Stir with a spoon.

Come up with wild names for landmarks in your pirate world.

Haunted Hills

2 Lay the dish cloth flat on a counter. Put the piece of paper on top. Dip the sponge into the tea water. Squeeze to wring out the excess water.

Rip the edges of the paper to show that this map has been around since pirate times!

3 Dab the sponge on to the paper. Continue until the whole paper is tinted brown. Leave to dry.

Make sure your treasure is well hidden.

X marks the spot!

Swashbuckle Stumps

5 When the paper is dry, use your felt-tip pens to draw a map of the route to the treasure. Choose a starting point, such as the back door, and mark the place where the treasure is hidden with an X.

4 Meanwhile, hide your treasure in a safe spot outside. If you are hiding food, such as chocolate coins, make sure it is sealed in a treasure chest (plastic container) so animals can't get it.

6 Draw extra landmarks along the route to help your treasure hunters.

7 To give the map an old-fashioned feel, crumple up the paper, then flatten it out again.

9 Give the map to the treasure hunter. See if they can find their way to the hidden treasure!

Forest of Doom

8 Roll up the map and tie it with ribbon.

Winding Way

VACATION CHAMPIONSHIPS

Why play just one game when you can hold a **whole sports competition**? Play different games and compete for **gold, silver, and bronze** medals for your team.

Running race

Set a starting line and mark a finish line at least 20 large steps away. Have everyone stand behind the starting line. Then, on your marks, get set, go... Race to the finish!

Opening ceremony

Divide your players into teams. If there are only a few of you, each of you could choose a different team name. Make a flag for your team and march around in an opening parade.

Tug of war

Find a long rope or jump rope. Divide into two equal teams. Draw a line in the dirt or sand between the two teams. Each team stands at opposite ends of the rope, gripping the rope tightly with both hands. On "Go," each team pulls as hard as they can to try to drag the other team over the line toward them. The team who does so wins!

Always be careful not to throw stones, even small ones, in the direction of other people.

Paper toss

Scrunch up pieces of paper into balls, or find some small pebbles. Mark a line on the ground with a stick, or draw a line across the dirt or sand. Stand behind this line and then throw your ball or pebble as far forward as you can. Make sure everyone else stands back! Mark where your ball or pebble lands with a flag or by scratching your initials in the sand or dirt. After everyone has had a throw, check whose ball or pebble flew the farthest.

Long jump

Mark a starting line on the ground with a stick, or draw a line across the dirt or sand. Take a running start. When you reach the line, jump forward as far as you can. Mark where you land with a stone or your initials in the sand or dirt. After everyone has jumped, see who jumped the farthest.

High jump

Find a tall tree. Stand below its branches and take turns jumping straight up. Who can touch the highest branch?

Closing ceremony

Award medals for each sport. Make gold (1st place), silver (2nd place), and bronze (3rd place) medals out of paper or plastic lids and string. You could also make special medals or trophies to give out awards for best sportsperson, loudest cheerleader, top team player, and whatever else you can think of!

PLAYERS
4+

RELAY RACE

Set up a **relay race**, then step it up a notch! Create extra challenges to test your team and **boost the fun**.

How to play

1 Divide into two teams.

2 Find a stick or make a baton out of a paper towel tube. Make one for each team.

3 Set up a starting line and another line on the other side of the playing area.

4 Line up in teams behind the starting line.

5 On "Go," player 1 from each team runs to the line on the other side and then back to the starting line while holding the baton. They must then pass the baton to the next player in line.

6 When player 2 has the baton in their hand, they run to the other side and back, and pass the baton to the next player in line.

7 Repeat until each player has had a turn. The team who finishes first wins!

Extra challenge

Invent new challenges for your relay race. Try these ideas to get you started:

• Each player must move in a different way. The first person from each team must skip, the second must run, the third must hop, and so on!

• Set up a suitcase of clothing or dress-up items at the far end of the playing area. Every time a player reaches it, they must put on an item of clothing. Repeat the relay several times so it becomes harder and harder (or sillier and sillier) to run!

What other challenges could you invent?

TAG TEAM

Try these variations on the ever-popular game of tag.
Run, run, as fast as you can!

Caterpillar tag

Start with one player who is It. When that player tags someone, they must join hands to become part of the It caterpillar. As more and more people are tagged, the caterpillar grows! Only the people at the front and back of the caterpillar can tag other players.

Tons of tag

If you have lots of players, you could split the caterpillar into groups so there are lots of little caterpillars chasing other players. Or, instead of joining hands, the tagged players could hold on to the shoulders of the player in front in a growing conga line. You could even play tag holding a soccer ball. If you're tagged, you must drop it and someone else can pick it up. What other versions can you invent?

FREEZE!

Freeze tag

Just like in regular tag, one player is It. When that player tags someone, they must stand still, frozen. Another player must touch them to unfreeze them. When all the players are frozen, choose a new It and start again!

Invent your own

Make up other types of tag. Maybe when the player who is It tags another player, that player must start dancing on the spot! They can't stop dancing until someone touches them. Or they could stand with their legs apart, and another player can unfreeze them by crawling through the tunnel. The trick is unfreezing others without getting tagged yourself!

HIDING GAMES

Are you **seeking** a thrill? Try these different types of **hide-and-seek games**, and then make up your own!

Can of sardines

In a normal game of hide-and-seek, one person counts while the rest hide. In this game, it's the opposite!

Choose one person to hide. Everyone else covers their eyes and counts to 50. The remaining person goes to hide. After the count of 50, the seekers must split up to go search. When a seeker finds the hider, they hide with them. Eventually, you'll all be cramped together like sardines in a can! The game ends when the last seeker finds everyone else hiding together.

Find a hiding spot that has enough extra space for people to join!

Invent your own

Think up new twists on the classic. Try these ideas to get you started.

Be the tree

Players must act like the object they're hiding behind, such as standing tall like a tree or curling up like a rock.

Moving target

Hiders can move to a new spot when the seeker isn't looking!

Sneaky spot

Choose a spot in the middle of your play area. While the seeker isn't looking, hiders can run and touch the spot, before hiding again. Count how many times you can touch the spot before being found!

HIDE AND FIND 👁️ 👁️

Instead of hiding a person, **hide an object**!
Choose a teddy bear or toy. One person hides
the toy while everyone else closes their eyes.
When the toy is hidden, everyone seeks.
The **first person** to find it **wins**!

You could also...

Add teddy bears or toys
Split into two teams. One team
hides a teddy bear or toy per
person. The other team must
then find all the teddy bears.

Add rules
Could you set a time limit for
finding the toy? Maybe people
need to search in pairs?

BRIIING!

BRIIING!

GETTING WARMER!

Add clues
The hider could give clues, such
as saying "hot" when players
are close to the teddy bear or
"cold" when they're far away.
Get descriptive, saying "as hot
as the sun" or "as cold as the
Antarctic!" when seekers are
super-close or super-far.

BOWLED OVER

Collect old plastic bottles and then reuse them for fun. Make your own **bowling game** and see if you can **strike it lucky**!

You will need
- 6 clean, empty plastic beverage bottles
- A clear, level space
- 1 small ball
- Sand, dirt, or pebbles
- Sticks, stones, or chalk (optional)

How to make

1   Pour a small amount of sand, dirt, or pebbles into the bottom of each plastic bottle to weigh it down. Close the lid tightly.

2   Paint or draw a number on each bottle.

3   Decorate the bowling pins with stickers and paint to make them look more realistic and fun!

How to play

1 On a flat surface, arrange the plastic bottles in a triangle as shown on the left.

2 Count about five large paces from the triangle's point. Draw a line with chalk or use a stick or stone to mark it.

3 If you're playing on a sidewalk, you could mark the edges of the bowling lane with chalk. If you're playing in the sand or dirt, you could draw a line with a stick. Or, skip this step.

4 Stand behind the line. Roll the ball using an underhand motion to try to knock down as many of the plastic bottles as you can.

STRIKE!
A strike is when you knock down all the pins at once on your first roll of a turn.

5 Take one more turn to roll the ball, then count how many bottles you knocked down in total.

6 Each player repeats steps 4 and 5. Continue for as many rounds as you like!

You could also add up the numbers on each bottle knocked over. These are your points. Whoever has the most points wins!

PAPER AIRPLANES

Take to the skies with your own creations. Make paper airplanes, then put them to the test. May the **best plane win!**

How to make

You will need
• Letter-sized paper

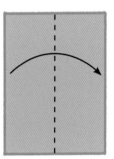

1 Lay the paper flat, with the short side at the bottom. Fold the left edge to the right edge. Crease, then unfold.

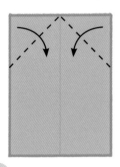

2 Fold the top corners down toward the center line. Crease well.

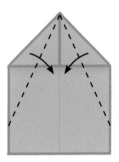

3 Fold the diagonal edges toward the center line. Crease well.

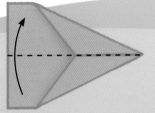

4 Rotate the paper so the tip points right, then fold the bottom edge up to the top edge and crease well.

5 Fold the top layer down so that the diagonal edge lines up with the bottom of the paper.

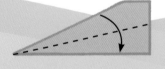

6 Turn the plane over and repeat step 5. Make sure the tip is pointy.

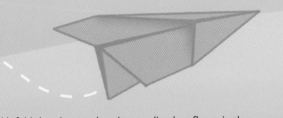

7 Unfold the wings so that they are lined up flat, grip the airplane beneath the wings, and let it fly!

Handy hints

• After every throw, press down on the creases and make sure the tip isn't crumpled.

• Try adding a paperclip at the front, under the tip, to give the plane extra weight.

• Never throw the plane toward a person!

TARGET PRACTICE

You will need
- Newspaper or letter-sized paper
- Different sized plates
- Sticky tape

How to make and play

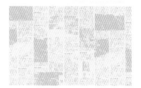

1 Use a large piece of newspaper, or tape pieces of letter-sized paper together to make a large sheet.

2 Trace around a large plate, a medium plate, and a small plate to create three circles, then cut them out carefully.

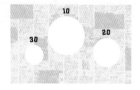

3 Write scores next to the circles. Give the smallest hole the most points and the biggest hole the least.

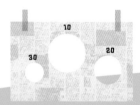

4 Use sticky tape to hang the sheet from a tree, soccer goal, or open doorway.

5 Mark a starting line several paces away. Stand behind the line and launch your plane, trying to get it through one of the holes. See how many points you can get!

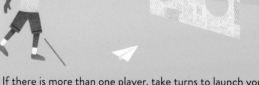

6 If there is more than one player, take turns to launch your plane. Let everyone have three turns, then add the points together for a grand total.

Distance challenge

For two or more players, mark a starting line on the ground. Take turns to throw your plane. Measure whose flew the farthest!

HOPPING HOPSCOTCH

Start with the standard hopscotch game, then build up **extra challenges** from there.

You will need
- Sidewalk chalk
- Area of sidewalk you have permission to draw on
- Pebble

How to make and play

1 Draw a standard hopscotch grid on the sidewalk with chalk, as shown.

2 Number the squares from 1 to 10.

3 Stand at the bottom of the grid. Throw your pebble onto square 1. If you miss, try again or pass the pebble to the next person in line if others are playing.

4 Skip over the square with the pebble and hop on the others all the way to 10 and back again. Hop on one foot for single squares. Jump with both feet for pairs of squares (e.g., 2 and 3).

5 On your way back, pick up the pebble and jump or hop onto square 1, then back to the beginning.

6 If you miss a square or step on a line along the way, your turn ends or you must start again.

7 Repeat steps 3 to 6, throwing the pebble on a higher number each time. You're done when you've cleared the grid for every number!

HOP TO IT!

Keep your balance for 26 winding squares!

Mix it up
- Instead of numbers, you could make an extra-long hopscotch grid using all the letters of the alphabet. Instead of tossing a pebble, see if you can make it all the way from A to Z without losing your balance or missing a square!

- Draw different shaped grids. You could draw a large flower with each petal numbered 1 to 9, and the center of the flower as square 10. Play in the same way as the traditional hopscotch game.

- Draw symbols or a different fun picture on each square. Then, instead of a pebble, call out instructions to each other. For example, you could say, "Two jumps to the sun!" The next player must then reach the square with the sun on it in only two jumps, jumping on any square along the way that they like.

HOP, SKIP, JUMP CHALLENGE

Draw a **long and windy game** along the sidewalk, writing instructions for different types of movements along the way. What **crazy challenges** can you think up?

Try these ideas
- Pat your head as you jump
- Side step like a crab
- Leap like a frog
- Dance backward

PICK UP STICKS

SIDE STEP

TIPTOE

CLAP HANDS

TWIRL

TWIRL

JUMP

RUN TO THE END!

FINISH

LEFT FOOT

RIGHT FOOT

SPIN

MOONWALK

BUNNY HOP

HOP

SKIP

MOVE LIKE AN ALIEN

START

HOP BACKWARD

MAKE YOUR OWN MINI GOLF

Go **crazy** with **crazy golf**! Use materials from around the house and the great outdoors to make your own creative mini-golf holes. Then **step up to putt!**

The basics

Mini-golf normally has nine holes. Decide what your holes will be and set them up.

Each person takes up to six shots to get their ball through the obstacles and into each hole.

You can keep score of how many shots it takes to get the ball in each hole, and add up the scores at the end. The person with the lowest number wins. Or you can just play for fun!

Start with easy obstacles. Make them more difficult as you go along! Here are some ideas, but you could invent your own, too.

You will need

- A small ball for each player, such as a plastic golf ball or ping pong ball
- A club for each player (toy clubs work best, or use a long stick)
- Nine empty yogurt containers or paper cups (for the holes)
- Recycled materials, such as cardboard boxes, tubes, and paper plates
- Items from the garden, such as sticks, buckets, wood, rocks, and a jump rope
- Pen and paper to keep score (optional)

Simple walls

Set up a straight course for the first hole. Lay a yogurt container on its side at the end, with the opening facing you. Use sticks or cardboard tubes to build walls along each side.

Swirl

Wind a jump rope into a spiral shape. Place a yogurt container on its side in the center. Get your ball around the spiral and into the hole!

Bridge

Lay a piece of wood across two upside-down buckets or large rocks to create a bridge. Your ball must travel under the bridge to reach the hole!

Monster

Cut arches out of each side of a cardboard box, leaving legs at each corner. Stick a paper plate or piece of paper on the front of the box and draw a monster's face on it. Stand your monster on the course to guard the hole, and sneak your ball under its legs!

Tunnel

Place a cardboard tube in front of a yogurt container. Have you got the skills to putt your ball through the tunnel?

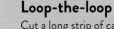

Loop-the-loop

Cut a long strip of cardboard from a box. Wind it around into a circle. Bend in the edges slightly so the ball has a groove to follow. Tape the ends down on the ground, lined up next to each other to create a looped path. You could also poke a stick through the cardboard and into the dirt or sand to hold down the ends. You might need a strong stroke to get the ball around the loop!

Windmill

Cut arches in the front and back panels of a box to create a tunnel. Cut notches into a paper plate to create a windmill. Attach the windmill to the front of the box using a brass fastener. Give it a spin before taking your shot. Can you get your ball into the hole without hitting the windmill?

The final challenge

Cut three different sized holes in a piece of cardboard. Label the largest hole 3, the medium hole 2, and the smallest hole 1. Lean the cardboard against a box and tape the top in place. Who can finish with the lowest score?

wAKEY
wAKEY!

PARTY GAMES

It's **party time**! When you've got a group of family or friends gathered together on your vacation, try these party games to step up the fun. **Make memories** playing and giggling through classic games and modern twists. Many of the games in this chapter work with smaller groups, too, and can be played indoors or outdoors. Guests of all ages can be involved, so **get the party started**!

VACATION CHARADES

How good are you at communicating without making a sound? **Test your talents** in this perfect party game for two players or a whole group!

FLYING?

SWIMMING!

CLIMBING!

You will need
- Paper
- Pencil
- Bowl or hat
- Timer (optional)

How to play

1 Tear a piece of paper into strips. On each strip, write a different idea to act out. Think about vacation locations, activities, and objects, such as the beach, camping, swimming, hiking, roasting marshmallows, playing a board game, etc. Place these in a bowl or hat.

2 Choose a player to go first. That player picks a piece of paper from the hat without showing anyone else.

3 The player must act out their word or phrase without speaking. They can use actions and common charades symbols to try to get the other players to understand.

4 All the other players shout out guesses. The first player to guess the correct answer is next up!

Playing a board game

Sailing

Climbing a mountain

Charades symbols

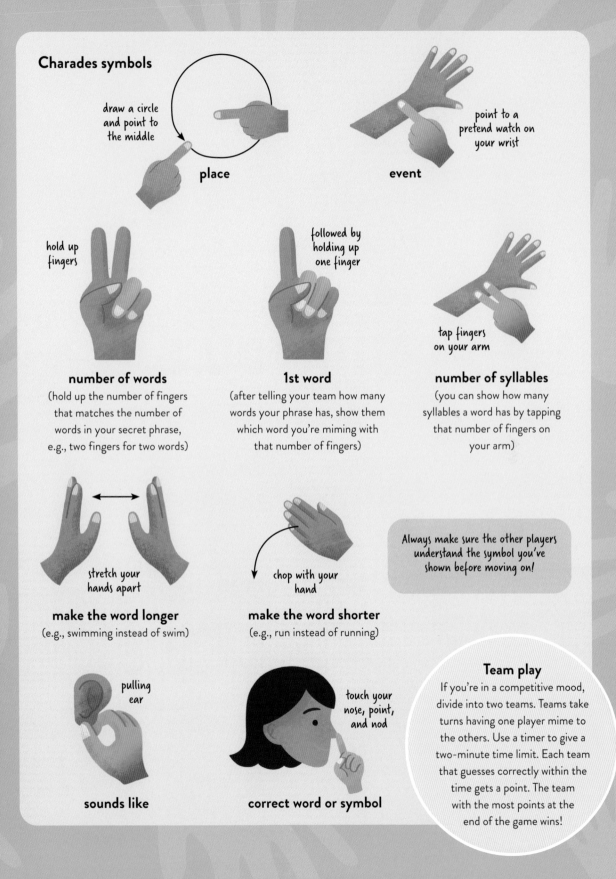

draw a circle and point to the middle

place

point to a pretend watch on your wrist

event

hold up fingers

number of words
(hold up the number of fingers that matches the number of words in your secret phrase, e.g., two fingers for two words)

followed by holding up one finger

1st word
(after telling your team how many words your phrase has, show them which word you're miming with that number of fingers)

tap fingers on your arm

number of syllables
(you can show how many syllables a word has by tapping that number of fingers on your arm)

stretch your hands apart

make the word longer
(e.g., swimming instead of swim)

chop with your hand

make the word shorter
(e.g., run instead of running)

Always make sure the other players understand the symbol you've shown before moving on!

pulling ear

sounds like

touch your nose, point, and nod

correct word or symbol

Team play
If you're in a competitive mood, divide into two teams. Teams take turns having one player mime to the others. Use a timer to give a two-minute time limit. Each team that guesses correctly within the time gets a point. The team with the most points at the end of the game wins!

123

GUESSING GAMES

Guessing games are a great way to **get the giggles going**. Try these challenges, then make up your own!

WHAT DID YOU SAY?

How to play

1 One player is the silent speaker. They move their lips to say their favorite part of their vacation without letting any sound come out of their mouth.

2 The other players must watch the silent speaker's lips closely to guess what they are saying.

CLIMBING THE MOUNTAIN.
CLIMBING THE MOUNTAIN.

3 The silent speaker mouths the same words over and over until someone guesses. (Or until you're all laughing so hard from funny wrong guesses that you can't guess any more!)

HIDING A FOUNTAIN?

SINGING AND SHOUTING?

HA HA HA HA HA HA HA HA HA HA HA HA

NAME THAT TUNE

How to play

1 Hum or whistle the first line of a song. Don't say the words!

2 Everyone else takes a guess. If another player guesses the song correctly, it's their turn to hum a song.

3 If no one guesses correctly after the first line, hum the first line again, and then the second line, too. Let the players guess.

4 Continue adding a line to the song until someone can name that tune!

ANSWERS AND QUESTIONS

How to play

1 One player thinks of an animal. They give clues in the form of statements about the animal.

2 The other players must answer in the form of a question beginning "What is...".

3 If a player answers correctly, in the question form, they're up next as the one to choose and describe an animal.

I LIKE WATER.

I'M BIG.

I'M GRAY.

WHAT IS AN ELEPHANT?

Act it out!

Add a twist with a forfeit! If players shout out the wrong answer, or answer without asking a question, they must act out the animal that is being described! Then the first player goes again with a new animal.

FOREHEAD FUN

Cinderella

The Beast

Gather a group and mingle around the room while playing this **silly guessing game.** Who will you be this time?

You will need
- Sticky notes (one for each person in the game)
- Pens

How to play

1 Sit in a circle. Every player should secretly write a fairy tale character on their sticky note.

2 Stick your sticky note on the forehead of the player to your left, without that player seeing what it is. Everyone should now have a mystery sticky note on their forehead.

3 Stand up and wander around the room, asking different players yes or no questions about your characters.

4 Look at each other's foreheads to see who others are so you can answer the questions.

5 Guess who you might be! Once a player has guessed their mystery name correctly, they remove it from their forehead.

6 They can stay in the game to continue answering other players' questions.

Rapunzel

Prince Charming

The wizard of Oz

Little Red Riding Hood

Sleeping Beauty

So many themes

Choose any theme you like for the names on the cards to play this game over and over again. Instead of fairy tale characters, you could try superheroes, storybook characters, or famous actors. For a travel theme, you could do places instead of people. Or what about using the names of friends and family?

Picture perfect

If you're playing with young children who don't know how to read, you could draw animals on the cards instead of writing names. Use animal sounds to help them guess!

If you don't have sticky notes, cut up pieces of paper and carefully tape these to your foreheads. Just be careful not to catch any hair in the sticky tape!

PICTURE PLAY

Put your **artistic skills** to the test in this game of sketching and guessing. Which team will **draw their way** to a win?

You will need
- Letter-sized cardstock
- Pencil
- Large paper or sketch pad
- Felt-tip pens
- Timer

How to make

1 Lay one sheet of cardstock on a flat surface, short side facing you. Fold it in half, bringing the left edge to the right edge.

2 Fold the top edge to the bottom.

3 Fold the top edge to the bottom again.

4 Unfold the whole sheet. Cut along the creased lines. You should now have eight smaller cards.

5 Repeat steps 1 to 4 using another piece of cardstock. You should now have 16 cards in total.

6 Choose four travel-related categories, such as Transport, Activities, Places, and Food. Write each of these on four cards.

7 On the reverse of each card, write a word that relates to the category. For Transport for example, you could have one card saying "train," one saying "car," one saying "airplane," and another saying "boat." For activities, you could write "swimming in the sea."

8 Repeat these steps to make even more cards!

Card front	Card reverse
Transport	airplane
Activities	swimming in the sea
Places	castle
Food	banana

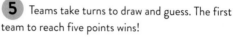

ice pop   train

How to play

1 Divide into two teams. Choose one team to go first.

2 One player from the first team stands at the front of the room with the sketch pad or a large piece of paper held against something sturdy to draw on. Make sure everyone can see the paper!

3 This player chooses a card randomly from the ones you made earlier. They announce the category to the room.

4 Start the timer for one minute. The player then begins drawing the word from the card as the others watch. This player's team must guess the word before the timer is up. If they do, they get a point!

5 Teams take turns to draw and guess. The first team to reach five points wins!

TRANSPORT!

TRAIN!

TIME IS NEARLY UP!

BUS!

Team B tries to guess what the drawing is.

Team A keeps an eye on the time.

Challenge
For an extra challenge, don't announce the category! Can your team guess what you've drawn?

tennis   apple

129

PAPER CUP GAMES

Anything can turn into a game! You might be surprised at how much fun you can have with the **humble paper cup**.

You will need
- Paper cups
- String
- Paper or coins
- Scissors
- Small stones
- Pencil
- Timer

TOSS

How to play

1. Use a piece of string to make a line on the ground.

2. Divide into two teams. Each team stands behind the line.

3. Place one paper cup three paces in front of each team.

4. Scrunch up paper into balls or use small coins. From behind the line, take turns to toss the balls or coins into your team's cup. Let everyone on your team have a go. How many can each team score?

5. Move the cup closer or farther away from the line to make this game easier or harder!

Put something heavy, such as a small stone, into the bottom of each cup so it doesn't tip over.

BUILD

How to play

1 Divide into two teams.

2 Set a timer for two minutes.

3 When the timer starts, each team builds a tower using the paper cups. Whose tower will be tallest by the time the timer runs out? And will it stay standing or come tumbling down?

What clever engineering will you use? A pyramid shape to strengthen the base? A one-on-one approach to reach higher heights? Give it a go and test your structure before you run out of time!

If you haven't got paper cups, you can try this game with rolls of toilet paper instead.

WHISPER

How to play

1 With a pencil, make a small hole in the bottom of two paper cups.

2 Cut a piece of string about 3 feet (1 meter) long. Thread one end of the string up through the hole in the base of one of the cups. Tie a knot to hold it in place.

3 Thread the other end of the string up through the hole in the base of the other cup. Tie a knot to hold it in place.

4 Stand in a circle, with everyone spread out about 3 feet (1 meter) apart.

5 The first person holds one of the paper cups up to their mouth. The person next to them holds the other cup up to their ear, pulling the string tight in between.

6 The first person whispers a message into the cup, then passes the cup to the third person in the circle.

7 Player 2 now whispers the message that they heard into the cup, with player 3 listening. Player 2 then passes the cup phone to player 4.

8 Repeat whispering and passing on the cup until it reaches the last person in the circle. They then say the phrase they heard out loud. Does it match what player 1 said at the start?

CAPTURE THE FLAG

You will need
- Colored cardstock
- Felt-tip pens
- Sticks
- Sticky tape

This game is best played **outdoors**. It's party-tastic when you've got lots of people to make up two big teams. Work together to **find victory!**

1 Make your flags

Divide into two teams. Cut a large triangle of colored cardstock and decorate it to be your team's flag. Give your team a logo or a cool symbol. Tape the flag on to a stick.

2 Setting up

Split the playing area into two sides. If you're in a playing field, you can choose the center line for the split. If you're playing on a beach, in a wooded area, or in a garden, mark the line with objects such as sticks or jump ropes. Each team then places their flag somewhere on their side. It can be partly hidden, but the other team must be able to spot it.

JAIL

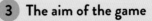

3 The aim of the game

The aim of the game is to capture the other team's flag without being caught. The first team to bring the opponent's flag back to their side wins!

4 Skill and strategy

Will you work together and travel as a team, or will you split up? Will you rely on speed and make a run for it, or go for a cunning hide-and-sneak technique?

Some more rules
- No moving your team's flag once it's been placed.
- Players must not stand within 3 feet (1 meter) of the flag or the jail while waiting for the opposing team.

JAIL

5 Seekers and guards

Some players on your team act as the seekers. They venture into the opposing side's territory to try to capture the flag. Other players stay behind as guards. They try to tag invading attackers from the other team.

6 Go to jail

Each team sets up a jail on their side. When an invading player is tagged, that player must go to jail. A player's teammate must tag them to free them from jail.

Family fun
You COULD split into evenly matched teams. Or, for extra fun, how about playing grown-ups vs. kids?

PIN THE PALM

You've heard of pin the tail on the donkey. What about **pin the palm tree on the desert island**? Make this vacation twist yourself, cover your eyes, and see who can **place the palm** in its special spot!

You will need

- Large sheet of paper or 4 sheets of letter-sized paper
- Felt-tip pens
- Cardstock
- Scissors
- Sticky tape or adhesive putty
- Scarf or bandana

How to make and play

1 Lay flat your large sheet of paper, or tape the four sheets of letter-sized paper into one large rectangle. Use your felt-tip pens to draw a picture of a desert island.

2 Draw the surrounding sea and a sunny blue sky. Add some sharks in the water, too! Draw an X on the island where the palm tree should go.

3 Have each player draw a palm tree on a piece of cardstock, color it in, write their name on it, and cut it out. Place a piece of sticky tape or adhesive putty on the back of each palm tree.

Winner!

4 Ask an adult for permission to tape the desert island picture to a wall. Blindfold the first player with the scarf or bandana. Slowly spin the player around three times, then position them facing the picture.

5 The player must walk with their arm out and stick the palm tree where their hand lands on the picture on the wall.

6 Each player takes a turn with the blindfold to place their palm tree. After everyone has had a go, decide which player's tree is closest to the X!

Teamwork time
Instead of playing to win, try a team game. One player is blindfolded as before. All the other players must work together with their words to direct the player as close to the X as possible.

CLOSER!

LEFT!

YES, THERE!

Invent your own
Come up with your own vacation version of this game. If you're at a pool, you could pin swimmers to a diving board. If you're traveling abroad, you could pin the airplane to your position on the map. Or think of an animal that you've seen nearby and pin on its tail!

DANCING GAMES

Clear space for a dance floor and get everyone **on their feet!** Play some tunes and move to the beat in these **groovy games**.

SWITCH IT UP

How to play

1 Choose one person to be the caller. Everyone else gets on the dance floor.

2 When the music starts, everyone starts dancing.

3 After a short time, the caller shouts out a dance move (such as funky chicken or the floss) or dance style (such as ballet, hip hop, or line dancing).

THE FLOSS!

4 Everyone must switch to that move or style and continue dancing in that way until the caller calls out something different.

5 The caller continues calling out new moves or styles every 20 seconds or so until the song ends.

6 At the end of the song, switch callers and play again to a new tune!

Some dance moves to try:

Alternate directions of arms and hips and see how fast you can go!

The floss
Clench your fists and swing your arms across your body, one in front and one behind. Move your hips in the opposite direction to your arms.

Slide
Hold your arms out wide. Take a big step to the side with one foot and slide the other foot to meet the first. Keep sliding back and forth.

Funky chicken
Place each hand under an armpit so your arms are bent out to the side like chicken wings. Flap!

Pirouette
Spin on one foot, with the other foot touching your knee, leg bent out to the side. Hold your arms out in front.

MUSICAL STATUES

How to play

1 Ask an adult to be in charge of the music.

2 When the music starts, everyone must dance.

3 When the music stops, everyone must freeze! The last person to freeze is out.

4 Continue playing until there is only one dancer left on the dance floor. They are the dancing queen or king!

You could combine this with SWITCH IT UP. Each time the music starts up again, the adult could call out a different move to do until the next time you have to freeze. How many silly positions can you hold?

CHOREOGRAPH A ROUTINE

How to play

1 Stand across the room in a line. The first person invents a dance move and shows it to the rest of the dancers. Everyone practices the move until they've got it.

2 The next person in line makes up another dance move. Everyone practices this one, too. Then put move 1 and move 2 together.

3 Continue with each player adding a new move to follow the ones that come before. By the end of the line, you should have a whole routine to perform!

WHO DID THAT?

Keep a straight face and your **lips sealed**.
Can you keep the **secrets safe**?

How to play

1 Choose one person to be the guesser. This person leaves the room and waits outside the door, listening for someone to sneeze.

2 The remaining players sit in a circle on the floor. Quietly decide among yourselves who will be the "sneezer." That person sneezes.

3 The guesser comes back into the room. They must guess who made the sneeze. If they guess correctly, the sneezer becomes the new guesser. If not, the guesser goes back out and tries again.

Make it harder
You could make the sneeze really high-pitched, or very looow.

COIN CHALLENGE

CHANGE it up with this hide-and-guess variation! When the guesser goes out of the room, one player takes a coin and clasps it in their hand. All the players in the circle hold their hands behind their backs, clasped as if they're hiding something. The guesser must come back in and guess who's ACTUALLY got the coin. Try not to give yourself away!

WINKING WAR

While the guesser is out of the room, choose one person to be the "winker." When the guesser comes back in the room, they must walk around the circle watching the players carefully.

Meanwhile, the winker must wink at other players. When you make eye contact with the winker and they wink at you, you must lie down "dead." You're now out of the game.

The winker continues to secretly wink at players while the guesser tries to figure out which player is the offender. If the guesser guesses the winker correctly before everyone is "dead," the guesser wins. But if the winker can wink at everyone before the guesser figures out their secret, the winker wins!

aHHH-cHOO!

Disguise your sneeze in a silly voice!

Invent your own
What else could you do to stump your guesser? Who made the animal sound? Who has the toy? Remember to take turns being the guesser, winker, sneezer, hider, and whatever else you invent!

CLASSICS WITH A TWIST

Gather a group of six or more people and play these **classic party games**. Then invent your own **twists**!

DUCK, DUCK, GOOSE

How to play

1 Everyone sits in a circle. Decide on one person to be It.

2 The person who is It walks around the outside of the circle. As they do, they tap each person's head in turn saying "duck," "duck," "duck," "goose."

3 When they tap a person's head and say "goose," that player must jump up and chase after them around the circle. If the player can catch the person who is It, that person remains It. But if the player who is It runs around the full circle without being caught and sits down in the tapped player's spot, the tapped player is now It.

The giant's keys

Try this GIANT-sized version of this circle-chasing game. Instead of having a player who is It, have one player who is the giant. They sit on a chair in the center of the circle of players. Place a set of keys under their chair. The giant closes their eyes. One player from the circle creeps forward to steal the giant's keys. When the giant hears the keys jingle, they can get up and chase the thief! The thief must dash through the gap in the circle (where they'd been sitting), run once around the outside of the circle, and return to their spot without being caught by the angry giant.

SIMON SAYS

How to play

1 Choose one person to be Simon. That person stands in front of the others.

2 Simon calls out an instruction, such as "Simon says touch your toes." Everyone must then touch their toes.

3 But if Simon calls out WITHOUT saying "Simon says," such as simply "Touch your toes," anyone who follows the instruction is out. The last person standing wins!

Step it up
Simon could say their instructions faster and faster. Who can keep up?

SIMON SAYS ROAR LIKE A LION.

SIMON SAYS DO A STAR JUMP.

GALLOP LIKE A HORSE!

SLEEPING LIONS

How to play

1 Choose one person to be the explorer. Everyone else starts the game as lions.

2 The lions lie down on the floor, as still as can be.

3 The explorer wanders around the room trying to wake the sleeping lions without touching them. The explorer could do silly dance moves, tell jokes, make animal sounds, or whatever else they think will make someone wriggle or giggle. When a lion moves, that person becomes an explorer and joins the first.

4 Who will be the last lion sleeping?

WAKEY WAKEY!

Step it up
Invent your own version of this sleepy game! For example, you could be sleeping bunnies in a field, or you could be statues frozen in a funny position. This is the perfect way to wind down after a busy day of partying and games.

NEVER STOP PLAYING!

Still looking for ideas? Now that you've made your way through the book, can you think of any other vacation games to make and play? **Get creative** with what's around you and think about what type of vacation you're on. Try these ideas to get your **creative juices flowing...**

Make a telescope out of a paper towel tube. Take turns looking through. What can you spot? Can you make up a story about the item?

Take turns rolling a dice. Who can roll the highest number? Call out a number before rolling. Can anyone roll that number?

Think of your favorite animal. Make a mask, then crawl, stomp, or slither around to act like the animal.

Blast some tunes and have a dance-off! Who can perform the wackiest moves?

Build a famous landmark out of recycled cardboard, tubes, and other materials around you. Make little characters out of cardstock or toys, then act out a scene!

WHAT ELSE CAN YOU INVENT?

MAKE YOUR OWN DICE

When a game calls for it, use this **template** to make a dice out of paper.

1 Place a piece of paper over this page. Trace the template onto your piece of paper.

2 Write a number from 1 to 6 in each square on your paper.

3 Cut out along the solid lines. Fold on the dashed lines to create a cube shape.

4 Use glue or sticky tape to secure the tabs in place.

You can use digits, dots, or even stars to show the numbers on your dice. Make it your own!

Photo Credits
The publisher would like to thank the following for their kind permission to reproduce their photographs in this book:
Key: t=top; b=bottom; c=center; r=right; l=left; bg=background

Elzani Smit: 3 br, 9 c, 89 c, 89 b, 92-93 bg 98 r, 100 r, 101 tl, 103 tr, 112 tr, 112 bl, 119 b, 125 r, cover bl

Duck Egg Blue Limited: 143 c

Getty Images: Tetiana Lazunova 42-43 bg, 80-81 bg; Manuel de los Reyes Rubio Garcia 100 l; Don Smith 102 b; Shawn Gearhart 120 r, 140 br; Alessandra Bucci 143 t

Shutterstock.com: Sergey Novikov 3 bc, 76 b, 97 br, 98 tl, 101 c, 116 c, back cover tr; Amorn Suriyan 3 l, 43 r; Robert Kneschke 3 r, 100 b, 106 bl, 109 b, 131 br, cover cl, back cover bl; Mr Doomits 9 br, 117 b; oliveromg 9 tr, 102 tc, 103 br; Purino 9 r, 101 tr, 13 tl; Manny DaCunha 10 r, 30r; stigmatize 10 tl, 16tr; Monkey Business Images 10 b, 22br, 49 tr, 51 br, 124 c; Lopolo 12 bl; BearFotos 26 r; Roman Samborskyi 27 b; Pressmaster 28 bl; Brian A Jackson 30 l; japansainlook 30 b; Pixel-Shot 31 tr; Prostock-studio 31 r; JPRFPhotos 31 tl; New Africa 32 r, 44 tr, 126 br; Rawpixel.com 32 b, 41 b; Levent Konuk 32 tl, 52 tr; Khosro 47 b; Sparkling Moments Photography 51 t; NadyaEugene 54 tl, 63 b; Elena Kharichkina 54 r, 61 tr; Olga Enger 54 b, 67 br; Hans Kim 71 br; Gelpi 73 b; Pasuwan 75 b, cover c, back cover br; Jeanette Virginia Goh 76 tl, 93 t; Karen Struthers 76 r, 81 t; Jacob Lund 98 b, 110 tr, 111 b; Milica Nistoran 102 tr; Tatevosian Yana 116 t; karelnoppe 120 b, 141 tr; JasaStyle 116 tl, 126 bc; Oksana Shufrych 122 c; ALEX S 126 bl; ellinnur bakarudin 131 tr; fizkes 135 r, 137 tr, 142 tr, 143 r; altanaka 139 tl; Hafiez Razali 142 bl